LOST VOICE

Discovering Life after Trauma and Abuse

Debbie Major

Copyright © 2017 Debbie Major
All rights reserved.

Printed in the United States of America

Published by Author Academy Elite
P.O. Box 43, Powell, OH 43034

www.AuthorAcademyElite.com

All rights reserved. No part of this publication may be reproduced, stored in a retrieval system, or transmitted in any form or by any means – for example, electronic, photocopy, and recording – without the prior written permission of the publisher. The only exception is the brief quotations in printed reviews.

Paperback ISBN 978-1-64085-038-5
Hardcover ISBN 978-1-64085-039-2
Library of Congress Control Number 2017908513

ENDORSEMENTS

Being lost with no voice is catastrophic in business or in life. The by product is often a lack of confidence and clarity. Author Debbie Major offers a fresh solution. She reveals a proven process for overcoming unwelcome abuse and reveals how to find our true identity and purpose.

Kary Oberbrunner, Author of *ELIXIR Project, Day Job to Dream Job, The Deeper Path, and Your Secret Name*

Debbie's book offers a 4-step model to help the reader deal with the fear of lifting the veil of secrecy on trauma and abuse. Her personal journey of discovery, forgiveness, personal growth and triumph are bravely documented for all to read.

Debbie has finally found her Voice. The book chronicles her story, her beliefs and offers resources in a well-written, easy-to-read, roadmap back to wellness. Not an easy story to have lived. Not an easy story to tell. Everyone has their own story. But we are the lucky recipients of this treasure box of help.

From childhood abuse to the President of multi-million dollar company, the reader has a lot to learn from Debbie's journey of success.

Marilyn Stewart, *Entrepreneur, trainer, motivator, innovator. A direct marketer. A voice for the customer.* Stewart Consulting Group, Author of *The Canadian Direct Marketing Handbook I & II*

DEDICATION

To my children whom I adore and if it were not for them I would not have had the courage to finally step forward and be heard. Ultimately so they would have a road map to follow of what love of self and love unto others looks like.

Special note to you the glorious reader as you travel towards healthy and whole.

To all of you who are about to embark on a journey of healing, self-finding and acceptance it is a new chapter and canvas of your life. A chance for sparkling new beginnings filled with hope, promise and a belief in self for the first time. We honour but close the old chapters in your lives and with confidence and drive you grow forward. Yes it is possible and yes you can. You do have what it takes.
I cannot wait to hear about your triumphs and jubilation and to help with your trials and tribulations. Anticipation of the celebration of bliss and happiness that comes with all the growing through the pain and hurt will bring.
Let us celebrate together.

DISCLAIMERS

Some names and identifying details have been changed to protect the privacy of individuals.

Names, characters, businesses, places, events have been changed. Any resemblance to actual persons, living or dead, or actual events is purely coincidental.

The Author has tried to recreate events, locales and conversations from over forty years of her life. In order to maintain their anonymity in some instances she has changed the names of individuals and places. She may have changed some identifying characteristics and details such as physical properties, occupations and places of residence.

Although the Author has made every effort to ensure that the information in this book was correct at press time the Author does not assume and hereby disclaim any liability to any party for any loss, damage, or disruption caused by errors or omissions, whether such errors or omissions result from negligence, accident, or any other cause.

The Author is not trained in the medical well-being field including but not limited to such things as a Doctor, Physician, Therapist or Councillor and is not part of any medical profession. This book is not intended as a substitute for any medical advice. The reader should regularly consult a physician in matters relating to his or her overall health and wellbeing.

A gentle and kind reminder to all that this is my story and if it were someone else's story the words would be different and so would the meaning. I encourage others to share their side so the world may hear their journey and their story. There is no one story or journey more important than others. The experiences and all that come with it belong in uniqueness to one owner. Each individual is qualified to tell their story and share the impact of it. I encourage that we all should do this as we all have a story in us to share that is only ours and ours alone.

CONTENTS

Introduction xv

Broken and Without a Voice

Journey of Alone 3
Invisible

Growing Up 8
Alone

Young Adult 33
Confused

For Better or Worse 47
Chaos

Carnage Left 56
Effect

Choices Made 70
Impact

Trapped Inside 86
Stop

Warped Reality 91
Bargaining

Break the Cycle 96
Hope

Building to Find your Voice

Courage 103
   To Get to a Safe Place

Love 105
   First to Understand Then to Accept

Anger 111
   Let it Go It Serves No Use

Emotions 118
   Stages of Grieving Loss of Self

Worth 126
   The Gifts Within

Prepare 131
   Of Sound Body Mind and Soul

Support 144
   That Special Person Place or Thing

Manage 148
   Share with Confidence and Purpose

Beautiful with your Full Voice

Alive Inside 155
   Begins With You

Anger at Bay 157
   Moving On

Gift of Voice 159
    With Purpose

Open to Receive 161
    Listen Hear Touch Feel Taste Smell and See

Find Ignite Share 163
    Other Missing Voices

Appendix A: Reflective Quotes 165

Appendix B: Charts and Resources 168

Lost Voice Group Discussion Questions 171

Acknowledgements 173

Documentation and Research 177

About Debbie 181

The Voice Within 183

There I was bruised and broken as could be
Aimlessly watching life drift by me
First came respect then total love of me
Miraculously when whole it is amazing what we see[1]

INTRODUCTION

My dream already exists and my version is the millionth creation no the billionth quite frankly it is the infinite creation. My dream is *on earth as it is in heaven.*

I have actually been learning and preparing since I was a child but I did not realize it until now some forty years later through all the trauma and abuse.

My whole life I have always said all of these experiences good or bad are for a reason. You place them in your hip pocket to draw upon later in life to help share show teach and guide. They are absolutely for some reason purpose or higher learning.

We all have a journey and story to exchange one that has been entrusted to us and only us. There is no one story one journey one person one cause better than another. We are all created equal. Every one of us is different and is to be celebrated. Every person has goodness within them and we can each learn from one another.

It does not matter whose story of trauma abuse or pain it is. Your story my story or someone else's story one act of torment or hundreds of acts of abuse like mine. They are all horrible and despicable. They mess you up in some way for life. More people than we think are living real time their own journey of anguish and all that comes with it.

Eventually it comes down to two choices break the cycle or shrivel up and die!

How we arrived from trauma, suffering, oppression, exclusion, bullying, harassment, self-doubt or other does not matter. It just matters that we did.

Arriving means realizing something is not right. Something is way out of line. This is not what life is supposed to be. To remain silent and down means never finding complete self or true reason for existing. Never having a say opinion or voice for fear of more agony, grief and shame or being mistreated is not the way to manage or go through life. Awareness, realization and acceptance begin the healing process. This is fantastic and needs rejoicing and celebrating. You have arrived.

I have a great family and have much love and respect for all of them. Recently I realized I have several saving graces my adorable lovable strong and honourable Mom, the voice of our Lord, my family and an upstanding group of friends. I was keen on my time at Sunday school and church until I was fifteen and my part-time jobs took me away. I joined the United Church of Canada in 1978. These collective early messages laid the basis of hope that allowed me to believe.

The impact of being mistreated is not understood fully today especially in children I believe. Each wound is different there is no nice one size fits all magic healing program. An area within our current system that needs more exploration, resources and government funding in order for Canada to create the best programs of wholeness for victims.

More help programs are needed that are tailored to and consider what type of treatment people may prefer. Such as more natural holistic or a combined treatment approach to create each tailored program would be beneficial. Not enough services are available for the most vulnerable in life or enough available that are reasonably priced government

INTRODUCTION

funded services. Even to know where to start looking for help never mind where to go is daunting.

The effect of the abuse growing up and on the decisions I made in life played a real part in how long it took me to gain confidence to be where I am today. A lot of time was spent in the cycle of warped and trapped. Deny, deny, and deny is a wonderful thing. Whatever gets you through the day or night is the phrase I go with.

In these times when I had no voice I lived only with my thoughts and I was resolved that no one could take them away. At the same time I realized I had to let go of the anger it does not help or serve any good in my journey to finding happiness triumph or having a voice. The resentment and spite that comes along with anger is not useful either.

Why do I let people injure me and do nothing? Why is there less problem and shame to charge a stranger? Why do we hide in shame? Why do we wait so long? Why are we so scared? There are more questions than there are answers.

Where there is a will there is a way learned and instilled from past generations or something within me or some of both? Spirit, grit and perseverance there is some of all this in me. I am a lucky one I came from a good environment. I cannot impress enough many do not. Through all of this I knew in my heart I have greatness in me. I am the opposite of common which is weird. If no one is common we are all unique and special then. It did take me fifty four years to figure out what that unique thing inside me was no worries I am right where I am meant to be. So with confidence intact I do not want to waste it or time any more both are way too precious.

Until you realize you are remarkable unique and have worth you will remain broken.

Why share? Who the heck cares? I care. People like me care. I do not want people to suffer with no voice for as long as I have. So I share raw and from the heart as best I can. My hope is to give better understanding about being stuck in what many professionals call the trauma – abuse insanity loop or cycle. I share so you can have a better understanding of what no voice and no name did to us in life. Coming to grips that the bad things that happen in life shape decisions we make and has impact on choices made.

It is not fair to be broken because your agony has sent you through crippling fear, numbness and silence. Many will repress their whole life and are managing or dealing with post trauma stress disorder and do not even realize it. Getting the right help is very important. Reaching a point in your life and seeing and feeling the control that a situation or person has on you is very difficult, devastating, scary and flat out wrong. No person has the right to control another person on this earth. We are in control of ourselves and no one else should force you or convince you otherwise. In a controlling situation you lose sight of how valuable you are and how worth it you are and you let the controlling figure manipulate you and that keeps you down the way the controlling figure in your life wants it. I spent a lot of time denying this control in my life. It is even harder to break free but I am here to let you know it is oh so possible and help to show the way.

With love of self and respect of self well intact it is okay to have an opinion and a say. Each and every voice in our lovely Universe matters including yours.

I am no different than anyone. I am not more outstanding than anyone. I am not. So why not share the ruts I spent many years in? I spend many years living in anger, spite and revenge. Why spend another day in the dark hole of abyss if my falls, stumbles, bumps and bruises can help?

INTRODUCTION

Scary you bet. Going places I have never been. But I am better and more worthy than what I have endured. Experiencing the great taste of liberation in accepting and loving all of me has left me thirsting and wanting more. This taste this feeling of being on the other side this freedom with no more torment and torture the beginning of true identity and raison d'être reason for being is electric. The hint of promise the pure magic life can be and it's worth your worth my worth leaves a sense of jubilation I cannot adequately express.

Up until now from this point forward a blank slate for the new who, what, why, where, and how for each of us to explore?

The time is now for step one. Growing towards fixing the broken you in order to discover and build the true you with cause on your way to beautiful you. Sharing your full voice with confidence and clarity for the whole world to receive without fear!

BROKEN AND WITHOUT A VOICE

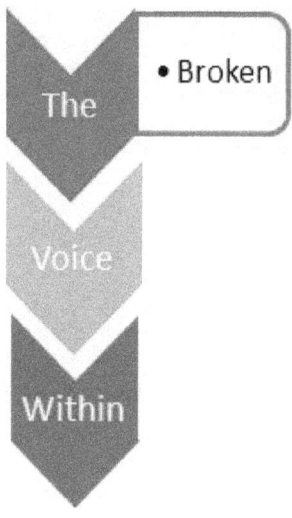

A home is where the heart is
a heart is where the love is
love is where we are
today tomorrow and always[2]

JOURNEY OF ALONE

INVISIBLE

When I was young my Mom would tell me I was a bold child. Even before the age of six I would call you up on things. What's that? Why are you doing that? That is not very nice. I would be up in your grill. Hence my Mom's reference at an early age to a bold child. That bold child went away at six years old when the misery darkness and bad acts performed upon me started and it took me until I was fifty four years old to finally stop the hurt and grief and be back to my Mom's definition of a bold child. By today's standards we call that a person who is confident with self and life.

I call it not being a door mat and wearing tread marks anymore. I am okay to let you know how I feel now. I do not live in fear anymore. I am okay to be seen and heard. I have the courage and the strength to share. It only took forty plus years to get here. It is a lot of struggle and uphill battles. It is the battle from within because no one sees the inner turmoil that is your life because you are a master of disguise.

I was fortunate and very blessed. I came from a house of love. Not all do. My Mom kept us safe sexually from the older generations in our family and extended family but she did not realize she had to keep us safe from the younger generations too. I never had the courage to tell. Some in my family today are still not aware.

My Mom wishes so much that I could have told her earlier of the sexual molestation I endured at the hands of others for over ten years. Too much fear I could not say anything. The battle within is ours alone so we think. No one sees the turmoil except us. We usually beat ourselves up for it pretty good too. We make sure we give it to ourselves from both sides and ends and we never cut ourselves a break. I wish too that she would have shared about the older generations in our family and some of their shameful acts. I believe forewarned is forearmed.

Pick a decade of my life the emptiness loneliness and loss of self I felt and lived and you would win. From childhood public school high school University work force and relationships friends and the list of people, places and things that caused pain go on. They seep out from the walls of life. There was much depression and most likely some undiagnosed post trauma stress disorder. I thought I had a good handle on things but as you grow and learn more each day I have come to realize I still repress a lot. To keep hold of all that pain serves no purpose really. There were hundreds of acts of abuse do I need to add to it by hanging on to it.

Do I wrack my brain trying to remember every detail? I ate so much disrespect for myself on a daily basis literally. Sometimes it would take me days before the shaking inside would stop. If you checked my hands they were trembling. Until this point there was not a period of my life that has not been without incident until now.

Some things you do not make the connection with until later on in life. Such as growing up being someone's little sister, someone's boyfriend, a wife it leaves you with a face no name and no identity. I was a bit of a loner and on my own a lot. At times I wondered in life does anyone even know I exist!

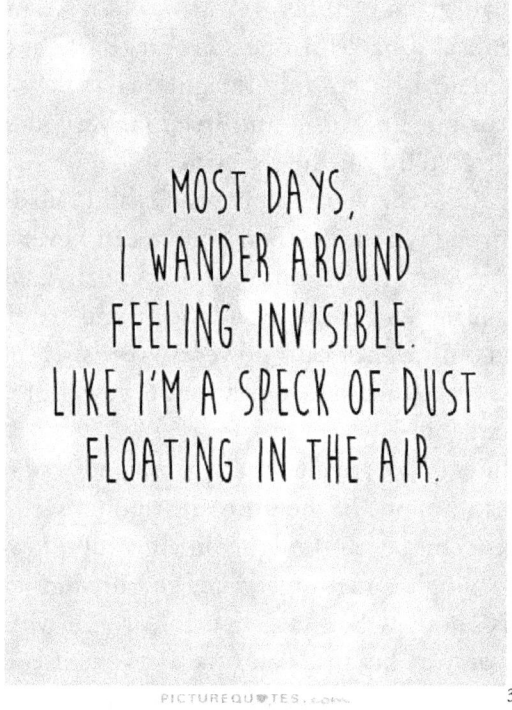

With self-worth in the toilet I never felt any sense of merit so I put up with a lot of things that were very disrespectful to me in silence. I took ate and endured all in quiet shame too embarrassed to tell anyone. How and who do you confide in? So I chose no one. I tried to hide things to appear as normal as possible to limit the noticing effect from others. But at what sacrifice? Alone nowhere to turn lost confused with self-doubt and zero confidence I was so afraid.

One's thoughts are very powerful. At times one's thoughts are all we have because we are stripped naked of everything else. We are raw and exposed all the time and it is a very vulnerable position. To make it work it was not a far stretch in my mind to imagine that at times thoughts would be all that a prisoner of war would have and many times that is all I had. Prisoners of war (POW's) endured far worse than I. I can only imagine what they suffered through for our liberation and freedom very sad and we are forever grateful for their sacrifices.

Many times the voice in my head is all I had and what got me through each day. Bad people can never take my thoughts away. They cannot steal them or have them. They are mine and mine alone. Seen and barely heard but armed with what I call "power of words" (POW's). In my head I linked prisoners of war and power of words as each remarkable.

Side lines of life are much safer a bystander an observer. And here in lies one of the problems? Being seen and not heard like a child even though you are a full grown adult. One day though something wakes you up and you think enough is enough. You take control of you, your voice, and your destiny because you finally realize if you do not you might as well plan your funeral on your way to that breakdown.

The dirt, stench and stink made me feel small little helpless useless like garbage a deadbeat a nothing. Some days you get close to going down that path again. The list goes on. So I chose to take the learnings and I let go of what serves no use. There is no need to be explicit in the hundreds of bad things that transpired in my life. For that absolutely is worth no justification. Instead to dwell on the healing and honouring of self and the strength to be heard and seen deserves our attention.

Being visible and heard is simply being. It took me a while to appreciate that we all have that which we need. We all have a gift that was bestowed upon us by the Universe the Divine or just because. Some will never realize what that gift is and that is tragic. Many will never be heard which is such a loss to the world. Self-esteem and lack of confidence is at the root. Without either is no way to go through life.

Growing and learning brings realization that all wounds bring meaning to life that will serve us well in future being and direction. These sores are not to weigh us down anymore. They do not serve any use other than to teach, share and help. More importantly letting go of the rage for it serves no point but to hold you back. Forget the past except to take the teachings. Honour where you and they came from, grieve that time of your life and may it rest in peace for ever more. Closing the past is for moving forward. I will not dwell anymore. I will show up and be visible in life.

GROWING UP
ALONE

I grew up the youngest of five with two older brothers and sisters. Fifteen years separates the oldest and myself. We grew up on the Quebec side of the Outaouais Valley and in the foothills of the Laurentian Mountains. My father was a Lumberjack in Northern Quebec his Mom was French and his Dad was English. He grew up on a Farmstead. It is still there today and in the family. I have many things of great history and importance from the farmstead and past generations. I am honoured to have my great great grandparent's love seat and single arm chair. These would have been by the fire at the homestead and would have been used most likely by the gentlemen after dinner. There would be no lounging in these chairs but you would sit upright with both feet on the ground. This love seat and chair are approximately one hundred and twenty years old. I also have some picture frames made by my Dad's hands from the barn board of the original family farm house from the late 1800's. My Dad's Mom was born in 1896 and I was blessed to have her in my life until I was sixteen.

My Dad would leave school at ten years old in grade four because his father died and he would have to go and help his Mom and family on the farm. Dad eventually bought a sawmill in the town we grew up in yet his day job was foreman at the biggest paper producing plant in the world at the time. The Canadian International Paper Company was the number one producer of newsprint in the world during its day. My Dad ran the plywood division. He had one thousand men and women reporting to him. He worked there for thirty five years never missed a day of work in his life. Serious job only was his motto. My two brothers would work hard for a living at the sawmill and my Dad worked full time at the paper mill and evenings and weekends at the sawmill. My Mom would help out too at the sawmill on the weekends with my Dad.

I am proud of my Dad for many things. In 1956 he built the home we grew up in with his own hands. Many of my brothers and sisters followed suit and built their own homes too. What a sense of accomplishment. Our family home was a twelve hundred square foot bungalow. Three bedrooms one bathroom and seven people in the house. Try that for a bathroom schedule today but somehow we managed just fine. The land cost three hundred dollars and the materials cost twelve hundred dollars.

There was one thing in particular I was extra proud of about my Dad. He was part of the team in Canada in the sixties that invented the two red buttons on heavy cutting equipment. In order that both hands and all fingers could be out of harm's way when the big blades came down to cut the product. In my Dads case the knives cut the long shavings that came off of the hot soaked log that when pressed together make plywood. He has taken many people with their fingers to the hospital to be reattached over his years at the plant.

My Mom would also leave school at a young age. She was twelve when her Father died. She had to go to work to help her Mom a widower with three small children. My Mom was the oldest. My Mom's Mom was only thirty six when she lost her husband. It was in the 1940s during the war. My Grandfather was home sick and passed away from pyuria of the gums. He would not have his teeth removed. My Grandmother hoisted their house up unto trailers and brought it from the country into town so she had a better chance for raising her three children and giving them a better life. A testament of strength and fortitude demonstrated by these earlier generations really is remarkable. My Mom's mom was born in 1909 and I had her in my life until I was in my thirties.

    My Mom was the oldest and at thirteen after her Dad died would take a train from the Quebec side one hour on Sunday nights to go to Ottawa to work Monday through Friday. She was a Nanny for a set of twins. She would watch and tend the children all week and on Fridays she would take the train back home. While in Ottawa she stayed around Mooney's Bay Park area. This was around 1942. In 2010 my daughter had a track and field meet at Terry Fox Stadium right by Mooney's Bay Park and my Mom joined us. It was an extra special day. It was wonderful to hear her share the memories of working in Ottawa both in the forties and again in the fifties when she was waitressing. I enjoyed the memories of the area and about how life in Ottawa was in the forties and fifties and the things my Mom would do for fun like swim at Mooney's Bay.

    She would go on to work with her Mom as a fourteen year old at the Singer Sewing Machine Factory in her home town. My Grandmother and my Mom had the best production record on the line. The sewing machine had wood parts. Some were about fourteen inches long and like a fire log. They would come off the conveyor and the men would run the belt fast hoping to create a pile of logs or a back log and shut the line down. The line never went down when the ladies were there. They were better than any set of two men that the plant could throw at them. I am so proud of my Mom and Grandmother. They are women from a different era. They were both a big part of the plant when all the men were away serving our Country in WWII. God bless all those men and women who fought died and are still enduring for our freedom today. If not for their sacrifice we would not be.

That is not to say this generation was not without its share of abuse. I cannot speak to my Dad's family but I do know there were forms of physical and sexual abuse in my Mom's family. Most of those generations are not here today to speak to that. My Mom has shared personal stories with me regarding the abuse in her family. She holds no grudges for these people or their acts of abuse. She is forgiving.

When I was two months old my Mom took a full time waitressing job at a Chinese food restaurant in our town. She worked evenings for thirty six years. She would leave for work at six thirty p.m. after supper, dishes and baths for at least three of us young ones. She would work from seven p.m. until close which was two a.m. on Monday, Tuesday and Wednesday and to four a.m. Thursdays and Fridays. After cash out and cleanup she would get home in the wee hours somewhere between three a.m. and five a.m. most mornings. She had to be up at six thirty a.m. each day to make sure that Dad and us children had breakfast and lunches for school. The two oldest were self-sufficient for breakfast. I believe at this time that one sibling was working and the other in last year of high school or at business college. If you can believe at breakfast time it was the one meal we could ask for whatever we wanted and Mom would make it for us. Some wanted eggs pancakes cereal French toast or toast with homemade jam or peanut butter. There was just one rule no bacon during the week. That was reserved for the weekend. She made breakfast for us with such love and joy not some days every day. She is beautiful.

If we were too young for school we napped in the morning and in the afternoon and my Mom would have a nap too. As you can imagine as we got older and did not need naps my Mom did not nap either. How she did that I will never know. I would have been sick, cranky and irritable. Not my Mom soft spoken and never angst just always so thankful for ability to be all together and healthy.

We spoke French and English at home. Before Kindergarten I would play with the children around my home and was able to pick up French easily one summer around the age of four. A young boy around my neighbourhood was French and I was English. When we played in the sandbox all summer by the end of it he was speaking English and I was speaking French. We never looked back. I would love to learn a third language too.

This would be what is called building new pathways in our brain which is an interesting learn regarding the great study of neuroscience. Learning new skills and getting out of your comfort zone builds new pathways in our brain even in adults. It is fantastic and is proven by many scientists. This is part of the healing process getting out of that comfort zone and doing new things or going to places you have not been before. It is very uncomfortable to be out of the comfort zone but it is a necessity. Fear knocks at the door each step of the way. It stirs up many emotions. It is easier to just abandon it. Why do we want to go there if it is so painful then?

One is not able to get to the other side if you do not go through the discomfort. Never quite getting to where you are supposed to be but oh so close. Always though once you get through it you inevitably say that was not so bad now was it. Come on you know you feel better when you do. We can all find something we do not want to manage in life but when you finally do you wonder why did it take so long to try? I had to get up enough nerve to manage letting people know. At first I did not do that so eloquently. I did a terrible job. Wrath, fury and distain oozed out my pores. I am in therapy to manage this disdain so I may let others know what happened to me and with therapy it will take me there faster and get me there deeper and with more meaning and love. I am honest enough to say to myself I am managing this now. It is no good to continue to lay blame for my disdain on others but to manage and meet it head on.

It was during this time when I was young I was old enough to remember my Dad calling me possessed. And this was because I would throw up all the time. If I was not busy and I got bored I threw up. I remember it starting young before school started and school started at five. I spent many summers on a lounge chair in the front yard with a bucket. If I stood up I threw up. I was also very motion sick. My Mom and I would run into Ottawa shopping and she would always have to bring what she called a "be sick bag". A be sick bag is a plastic bag with a towel in the bottom to absorb the liquid and so it did not make noise if you needed to be discrete in public. Complete with a face cloth to clean up. Moms have big hearts. For me I think I had a sick stomach because it is about being connected and feeling everything in Universe through my sensitive stomach, heart and body. After kindergarden and grade one Dad said "Mom you should bring her to the Doctor."

My Mom always remarked for a little country Doctor she like our local Doctor. He said to my Mom "my dear woman this young girl needs to be kept busy." And so being the youngest of five and not a lot of disposable income my Mother set about to find all the free things that I could participate in. Sunday school was a given and with extra church outings my bouts with throwing up slowed down. I joined Canadian Girls in Training (CGIT) when I was old enough I went to bible study I joined Brownies at seven and when old enough I joined the junior choir at church. This helped. I taught Sunday school as a young teenager. I was a Girl Guide a Ranger and then a Pathfinder. I earned my All-Round Cord in Guiding. I started ballet and modern jazz lessons at twelve because of my cousin and I liked swimming lessons at the local YMCA as well and earned my bronze medallion at the age of fifteen.

As a family we took pleasure in going to camp for summer vacation and I have fond family memories of fishing swimming having family bon fires and sing songs. During the winter months whoever was not working and around would go cross country skiing. It would take the group of us all morning to climb the mountain. At the top you would take a retreat. There was usually a nice log cabin with a roaring fire. We would pack thermoses of soup with sandwiches have a beautiful meal and set off down the mountain after lunch. The decent would take us no more than thirty minutes even if Mom had to sit on her skis because she would get going too fast. Skiing for my Mom as a young girl was her only way to get around some winters. It was nothing to slap on a pair of boards with string and ski ten miles to see a friend. Today it is Mom can you drive me to my friends please?

My older brother is fifteen years older than me and he played hockey and fastball so as a family we followed him every weekend growing up to many tournaments right up to my twenties. My Dad sold the sawmill where my brothers worked but having worked with wood my oldest brother went on to have a successful business supplying kiln dried wood to the furniture industry across Canada. Coming from this background it is easy to see why my Dad rests in the ground in an urn from a special Japanese tree that does not decompose for one thousand years.

My older sister is ten years older than me and was a majorette in her day. My Mom would take my other sister and I to watch her in parades in Ottawa many times. My sister could twirl and throw that baton really well. She is this cute adorable bundle and stands just over five feet tall. She was the first cheerleader of the family at our high school and my other sister and I followed in her footsteps and joined the cheer team at school when it was our turn. My Mom sewed our high school cheer uniforms for all three of us girls and helped us make pairs of homemade pom-poms with phentex wool. She is still this gorgeous tiny package of beauty and joy inside and out and you just want to pick her up and protect her. She would attend Business College referred to as secretarial school back then. She would climb the ladder to the highest administrative level within our Federal Government as an Administrative Assistant Level Seven referred to as an AS7. She realized that the engineers she worked for were brilliant but without her the department was a logistical and administrative mess. She had a boss that reminded her she belonged at the table just as much as the scientists and engineers did. That without her the functioning of the department would suffer. From this she understood her merit, value and worth. This story my sister shared resonates with me still today because often we do not realize our value or worth enough.

I have a sibling in the middle my brother who is seven years older than me. He has a tender heart. He is so kind and giving that people do tend to take advantage and exploit this in him. He worked for the family sawmill for many years and delivered many loads of lumber. Today he is an excellent long haul truck driver and you can catch him running the Ottawa Toronto corridor five nights a week. You would think with all that driving in his spare time he would not want to drive anymore. But there is something about the open road in our family and this brother has always had an RV trailer and currently hauls a fifth wheel and explores Canada and the United States with his wife.

I have a sister who is two years older than me. She is retiring this year after thirty five years of teaching grade four students. She has so much patience compassion and love for the children she teaches. She enriches everyone who has the grace to be in her presence. She is the true effect of patient and calm. She has love for her family and for everyone too and a kind and warm heart. All my brothers and sisters do. They are all married make great husbands and wives and have beautiful children to which I am very proud to be their Aunt.

There is a special person in my life and we are like two peas in a pod. We went through many similar atrocities growing up. I hope she realizes how beautiful she and her soul are. I pray for her that she has a chance to tell her story as it would definitely bring healing to many who hurt in this world.

Each of my siblings like our parents enjoys the act of giving freely. My brothers and sisters have been and still are members of their respective communities at large. This has been instilled in their children too and is a great thing to see.

The family setting saved me. Many are not saved. Many are lost for ever. Personally my goal is to save more. I feel I must make sure everyone is aware of the beauty within. Today a ninety two year young women said "you must take the bitter with the better." She is right the acts of brutality were bitter but the beauty of growing to accept oneself just the way we are outshines and is worth the fight and agony in getting here. I imagine there will always be a bit of bitter with the better.

I had started dance in the first year of high school. In grade nine you could try out for cheerleading and it seemed like a good fit. A great way to escape and I would not have to talk to people, not be in school and not be in class. What a great way to hide and run away. At our high school there was a junior and senior varsity sports team but only one set of cheerleaders. The cheerleaders were out of class at least for two afternoons a week maybe more if the basketball season crossed over with football. Queen of running away in a crowd I am I am.

I was embarrassed by my parents back then. They were older and not cool. They were not educated. It was not until later in life I realized just how much my parents had done and accomplished with so little and I am very proud of both of them today. Back then many of my friends had parents just about the same age as my older brother I could not relate to the average family or so I thought. My families' thinking was old school or just different.

As kids we would go to the sawmill on the weekends. We would look for pop bottles that the men might have left while working there during the week. My sister and I were allowed to collect and bring them to the corner store for a refund and ultimately for candy. We could amass quite the haul of penny candy in a small brown paper bag. We thought in the late sixties we invented the all-dressed potato chip by mixing a small bag of vinegar and barbeque chips together which we could do if the haul of pop bottles was enough.

Sometimes we would go in the big trucks to deliver wood with my older brother. I sported a short pixie haircut with a stubborn cowlick bang. It was not uncommon to hear the customers say "you brought your little brother to help you." My brother would say "no this is my little sister." I am sure he said my name sometimes but most times I just heard little sister. My family would not have known at that early age the impact that might have had on a person going through trauma nor did I at that time.

All of these are like bread crumb clues to the lost identity. I am not sure who in my family gave me my nick name but at six I was Sammy or Sam. I was more a tom boy than a girl growing up. I liked to be outside playing with the wild cats or playing meat butcher and wrapping up sand as hamburger in newspaper or riding my bike to a place we called blue berry mountain. A place where there were lots of blue berries in the summer and a great toboggan hill in the winter. I had the wind knocked out of me for the first time one snowy day at the bottom of that hill. My stomach met friends feet and voila wind knocked out of me.

Lake Beauchamp was very close to where we grew up too. It was an excellent source of fun for kids. A place to swim with lifeguards in the summer and a place to skate and cross country ski in the winter. Growing up in the summer after the chores were done at the house my Mom would walk us all to the beach for afternoon fun. She instilled early in us if we all helped and pitched in with chores we could all get to the beach earlier. If we all helped in the world and pitched in we could all realize a better quality of life sooner too. If we all share the load is easier for all.

It begins in earnest with offering value or help for free to our family, neighbours and community because we want to not because we have to. I remember dusting with a tea towel and pledge around the age of five so we could go to the beach in the afternoon. The seed to help is solidly planted and encouraged.

My Mom was an elder in her church for fifty eight years until she moved to her senior living center. She helped many people in our community. She knitted mitts, hats and scarves for the nuns in our town who helped those less fortunate especially the children. If we walk our home town in the winter I can still find children wearing the knitted mitts, hats and scarves my Mom made. As part of the church the Woman's Group accomplished a lot of fundraising for those in need in our town. This group is still active today.

My Dad played the fiddle and the mouth organ and coming from Quebec he could call a mean square dance. So we were always piling into the car and heading off to a barn dance or a square dance. Four of us kids play guitar and love to sing. We had a chance to do this with my Dad and Uncles that played. We did this at quite an early age and all through our lives especially once I had the confidence to master singing in public and playing guitar at fourteen. My Dad was born in 1925 and my Mom was born in 1929. They lived the dirty thirties the time of food stamps and food rationing. My Dad received his letter to report to army boot camp when he turned eighteen. Again so blessed the war ended three weeks later and my Dad did not have to go. The years of birth for us five kids are 1948, 1952, 1955, 1960, and 1962. I only share this with you to show the generational spread in our family. Many kids my age had parents just a bit older than my oldest siblings. So growing up I quickly separated family into old generation and new generation. Just the thinking of both generations is very different in regards to risk aversion and playing it safe versus taking chances. As well as what gets swept under the carpet and forgotten and what does not? The older generations tend to want it swept under the carpet. It translates to different views on many different subjects and levels.

I can only imagine for those that do not have such a solid foundation how hard the struggle and turmoil is. Arriving becomes harder without solid foundations but not insurmountable. Since my eyes heart ears are wide open I see and feel a lot of pain coming from ones with splintered shattered beginnings. My heart aches for those who are hanging on in life not knowing they are the valuable one that they are what matters. Not realizing they are not scraps or a cast away of life they are human beings with faces names and feelings.

In grade one I wanted to take skating lessons. Some of my friends at school were taking skating lessons. So my Mom enrolled me. With only one car that meant I had to take a different school bus at the end of the day. I do not remember how I did that. I took the school bus that went by the local arena not the normal school bus I took home. I had been to the arena many times to watch my older brother's hockey games and for public skating. I knew where the changing rooms were. But never had I been there alone. I got off the bus went into the arena put my skates on and then realized the ice was so big. It was divided into groups. I could not find my group. Somehow I did. My Mom would come to the arena and pick me up after I was finished. By this time my Dad would be home from work and have had supper. My Mom would get the car before she had to go to work and would come and pick me up. I managed this only three times. Each time I got to the ice I was so scared to ask for help to find my group I did not go back. It was overwhelming. The tricks I can do on skates today come from those three lessons. I wonder what would have happened if I had the courage to stay that whole session? Not bad for a six year old exhibiting drive even at that early age.

The bad dark stuff had just started I was around six years old. At first a teenage boy in our neighbourhood pinned me against at the church across from our house against that cold light tan smooth brick. He was fifteen he felt me up and down and lifted my skirt and pulled my panties down a bit as he pressed against me. He asked me why I had underwear on. I ducked and snuck out the side along the wall and ran home too scared to tell anyone.

It can also be as innocent as during public school being placed beside all the bullies rowdy kids or class clowns. I was the quiet little mouse so maybe my habits would rub off on the rambunctious kids was the thought process. That is how the teachers explained it to my Mom and then my Mom explained it to me. But no one thought to ask why I was so quiet?

The child I was beside in grade one picked and poked me most of the school year until I could take no more and I cut his hair with scissors in art class that spring. Of course I was disciplined. But my Mom and the teacher shared a good laugh I found out years later.

This incident is so much in contrast to my Mom's strength and courage. One day when she was in grade two she came upon a grade six boy. He was sitting on the chest of a grade three boy and pummelling his face in the school yard during recess. She removed the grade six boy from the younger boy's chest. Threw him down on the ground sat on his chest and pummelled his face. Later that evening the Mom of the grade six boy came to my

Mom's house. My Grandmother answered the door. The woman wanted to see the big boy who had beaten up her boy. My grandmother was confused? She told the lady I have no big boy. My Mom was her eldest child and her boy was only two years old at the time. My Mom never told her Mom she beat the grade six boy up and the grade six boy never told his Mom it was a girl in grade two that beat him up. My Mom is still so strong in character to this day. Two generations so different. In comparison I would remember to not ask questions in class or try very hard to just exist or be without being seen or heard. Do not make waves do not ask questions do not stand up for what you really want and pray in school no one calls upon you to answer anything.

One day early on in public school the teacher said "no more going to the washroom." Everyone was taking a turn and the teacher was disrupted one too many times. We were young enough the washroom was within the classroom. I had to go very badly but teacher said "no one can go." I did not have the courage to let her know so I urinated in my pants. The teacher made me clean it up in front of everyone. I had to wipe and clean my wood blocks under the desk and all. It is mortifying and part of the formative years and the feeling of sad sets in. That event is forever burned in my memory. A class of school mates watching you clean up and even if you work your fastest it still takes ten minutes too long of burning eyeballs. I was ridiculed in the school yard for years to come. Another child is lost degradation sets in and no one has the foresight to ask any questions or see that something is wrong.

Right on its heels begins the sexual assaults maybe they were earlier but I still repress as I endured this for a period of ten plus years. I thought I had a pretty good handle on events but as you put your life under a microscope things pop up unexpectedly that trigger an old or new memory and all those horrible feelings come back. The people who hurt me the most were extended family so when you were going to family functions it was not like you could say "sorry Mom and Dad I am not going" or "Mom can I stay home?"

Sexual groping inappropriate touching inappropriate language being penetrated and raped before fourteen is not the way a young person should grow up. It is something no one should ever have to deal with or go through in life.

In grade three we took a bus to and from school. *The Partridge Family*[4] was a popular television show at the time. There was a song "I Think I Love You" on the show and the whole bus would sing it to me but change the words to "We Think We Hate You." At eight I could not figure out what I had done to them. I could not tell you how that makes one feel. I was a real loser a nobody in grade three. I remember I was staunch I did not cry on that bus I just looked forward. I was the weak link I guess so it made for an easy target. How do people smell the weak ones out? My sister does not recall these events on the bus but I do.

Sexually assaulted by a boy in public school there were several incidents. The kids at school did not know anything about these happenings between us but I knew. You wear the big L for loser like the scarlet letter around your neck. It is your chain and cross to bear. You are convinced everyone can see feel and read your shame and worthlessness anyway.

One rainy day you know the ones when the whole school plays inside in the gym. This was a small school and had approximately two to three hundred kids. Someone tells me my boyfriend is outside I go out to see. It is the boy who has been assaulting me. I grab onto the front door from outside the school. I am in my rain boots and hat and I pull on the front door. There are five people holding the door on the inside not letting me in. My foot in my rubber boot slips and goes through the big glass pane of the front door. I shatter the whole glass front door of my elementary school. Every kid tries to empty from the gym up the stairs to the lobby. As close as they could get jammed in to see what the commotion was about. Deer in the headlights the whole school is looking at you and you are frozen, numb and all alone. More ridicule with shame sets in. I was disciplined at school with detentions but my parents did not have to pay to have the glass replaced in the front door. For the next few days until the large pane of glass was repaired the boarded up window was there for the school to see and so was my disgrace. Little did anyone know for me it was the dirt of the sexual assaults by the boy outside the door at school that is all I saw and I was mortified!

By the time I turned twelve starting high school I was in with a bit of a mixed up crowd. We all came from decent families but were exposed to a lot along the way. Some families a bit more dysfunctional than others but then aren't we all? Once we got to high school with all the public schools feeding into it I did not hang a whole lot with the kids from my own public school because I did not hang with them a lot outside of public school growing up either. I was never invited and I lived far from the kids I hung out with at school. My parents had one car so I hung with kids from around my neighbourhood who spoke French and English. I hung with some kids from my public school around my house but not the kids that I hung with at school and I played with some kids from the French school system around my house growing up too. Once I got to high school there was a lot of splitting up of groups and finding new groups to hang out with. I did not exactly make the right choices all the time and I no longer wonder why. I gravitated towards the groups I knew I would be accepted in. Not always the best choice I could have made. Here in lies the feeling of floating invisible through life.

High school was no cake walk either. It was very hard. I was shy. Many confused this with being a snob. Too scared to keep my head up I would look at my feet. If I kept my head up someone might ask me something or talk to me and what would I say? They might say hi? What would be my answer? So I looked at my feet all the time. This was real for me. I would throw up most days knowing I had to walk across the cafeteria school floor. So many eyeballs on me and I was too afraid to look up. Today I not only look up but I soak in what I see. It is a beautiful world out there it is simply amazing.

A lot of people in your circle will not understand this because they have not lived the compound interest effect of suffering day after day like many of us hurting have. Most common phrase I hear from people is "get over it." Unless you have lived it you can only think you know what it is like to eat garbage. If you are already a confident person perhaps it is hard to see or visualize this which is the other end of the confidence spectrum. Definitely more awareness is needed.

In Quebec high school starts in grade seven and ends in grade eleven this is called secondary one through secondary five. Grade seven, eight and nine are the juniors in high school and grade ten and eleven are the seniors. With seniors coming back for victory laps and late birthdays you have twelve year olds like myself with eighteen to twenty year olds. It did not take long at high school to get in with the wrong crowd and doing the wrong things. In the fast lane to nowhere drifting with no arrival date in sight!

It was around this time I started living at my friend's house and slept there most nights of the week. My parents asked me where I lived and I said "my friends." No one ever stopped me or asked why? My friend was in my grade and her sister and friends were two years older. My friend had a younger brother too. We hung with the older crowd. This was a caring house a safe house. I know now if I was there the bad people could not find me to hurt me. You have to outsmart the bad people to survive. Thank you to whomever for giving me strength to formulate in my subconscious at a young age. I should have confided in my Mom. This is a common thread that rears its head throughout. I encourage everyone have that chat with someone get things moving for sake of your existence. My friends' Mom was a single Mom and wanted her kids to be safe so it was not uncommon to have a dozen kids there at any given time with three or four sleeping over. I was one of them who slept over. Many kids stayed at my friend's house over the years.

I am the baby of the family and really got away with a lot. Spoiled you could say. I appreciate what I was given with much sincerity. My Mom took thalidomide during her pregnancy for me and she was worried for my arms and hands hence she never could spank them. Although she never had too her words were always enough. My parents had seen it all by then what new trouble or adventure could I get into that they had not already experienced before from my four siblings that came before me? So many barriers were already torn down for me such as curfew. I never had one. So to say I was going to my friends to a party and stay all night was not unheard of. One morning we are all crashed at my friends after a party and someone sleeping over wakes up in the morning and pressed his naked body against mine and he pins me down. I do not know how to push people away? Another house party someone else pins me down and again how to get out when one has no courage. How do you get out of a bad situation when you just do not have the capacity to do it? No one cares or even notices and at fourteen you do not have a lot of life figured out. This is definitely one still frame of what zero confidence looks like in a person's life. Must a whole reel of still frames be created before we collectively wake up?

It was grade nine in high school and I went on a ski trip for a week. I thought it would be a good way to get to know other people from my school. I had snuck alcohol from my parents for the trip so I was popular for some of the ski trip until it ran out. Then one of the girls from my school did not realize I was in the room and she swore saying "what the bleep is she doing here?" She was referring to me. I stood up tail between my legs never acknowledged it did not cry walked out and hung with people from a different school than mine for the rest of the week. Back at school for the next while I got the cold shoulder from the ski trip group. Good thing I always liked me myself and I they are often all I have or so I thought. Again what did I do that people want to exclude me. Of course I never had the confidence to ask or find out. Someone with no confidence is visible to other people in your mannerisms and body language. I see now that if you give off the smell of weak then that is what other people read off of you too.

I skipped and or missed a lot of school if I was not there I could not get picked on. Or if I was in class my mind really was not there. How easy it was to miss a class. I was very good at forging Mom's signature so a quick note to be excused could be whipped up when needed. Like when you knew there was going to be group work in class or potential to have to stand up and speak. I could telephone my Mom and ask once in a while if I could go with other friends who were off to attend an event during school hours. Most often she would say if my work was done I could go. I would just skip class because I did not feel like going. If I knew I had the propensity to be called upon I would evade and sit under one of the big pine trees at school. One day the Vice Principal stopped me leaving school at the end of the day and he said "I saw you today and if you are going to do that tomorrow do not bother coming to school." I went to school and I did not skip any classes the next day. I never failed anything in high school and I was in the academic stream. We had an enriched and an applied stream in school at the time. I never liked classes I might get asked something and be made a fool of the way I was in public school so I avoided most classes like the plague. I do however like knowledge and learning.

We had to go into the office to pick up our report cards at the end of the term or school year. The Vice Principal handed them out and you signed for them. He looked at every report card for each of us eighteen hundred students. He looked at mine for that year fifty three absences in chemistry and I earned a mark of fifty one. I am not sure about your school but in mine if a teacher liked you and you were border line you would get a fifty one. If they were not so fond of you or you were a trouble maker you received a forty nine. Fifty was the pass and up until grade nine or secondary three anything over a mark of seventy five you were recommended and that meant you were excused from writing the final exam. No such recommendations in grade ten and eleven. Our Vice Principal looked me straight in the eye and said imagine what you would have gotten had you have been there the whole term. He is right but he did not realize I was running at the time no one did. Even in this environment of education and learning no one asked why I missed fifty three classes of chemistry. This was in the late seventies. Today this is my go to question now that my eyes are wide open. I always ask why someone does that action or says that or feels that way or looks that way. I try anyway as best I can to find out why?

Here is an aside some trivia you might say. But lends itself to the uniqueness of Canada which is part of understanding our great uniqueness and differences too. In the province of Quebec in order that your child receives education in English one of your parents must have attended English school in Quebec. I have a certificate from the Government of Quebec from 1974 giving me the right to attend English school in Quebec. During the thirties my parents attended the Red School in a little town called Thurso. It was a one room school house with grades one through seven and instruction was given in English. This earned my siblings and me the right to attend an English school. I have nieces and nephews in Quebec some attend French school and some attend English school. This rule still applies today. I have only visited Europe once but Quebec is a culture onto its own and one of the things that makes that province so unique. Of course all of our other provinces and territories are unique and special each in their own way. I have not visited Newfoundland or the Territories and cannot wait to visit them one day to feel and see their uniqueness too. They are special just as we all are.

I was left out of a lot of things when I was young or better yet just not included. No one gave me a second thought. None of my friends telephoned the house for me ever. No one called to ask if I wanted to join them. You learn very early on that you had to say things like "I will meet you at 2 pm" otherwise if I asked to join them I would be volleyed back with why the heck would we want you there? Well doesn't that make you feel wanted in life? Who wants a deadbeat loser anyway? No one that is who!

Everyone says I am a loser so I must be one then. Now I realize the so called everyone in my life I was concerned about and listening to is really no one that can affect me. Their crank and misery on life is really about them not about me. They are lost souls themselves just like I was and they need help. However I cannot worry for everyone and I cannot let their thoughts and beliefs about themselves control my destiny.

During this time growing up I experienced a general sense of emptiness sadness and crying all the time. A sign of depression I am sure. I cried in private where no one could see or judge me. I attributed my highs and lows as emotions and feelings. Super high part of a day super low the next minute too young to know why? I felt like the second long lost cousin. I felt inferior dirty like garbage. I was a low life a throw away. Your thinking gets warped. These are formative years and you think this is normal this is what life is supposed to be. No one asked or no one saw anything. After awareness and arriving we see everything we become way more intuitive to people who are suffering.

You are numb have a sick stomach most of the time a headache and a big permanent lump in your throat. So you try to rise above as best any young person can. You try to make sense of it. You put that chin up and you lead with it head held high. You try and rise above the horrible names and feeling of emptiness and you try to get yourself into healthy situations like dance, drama and cheer. I also picked up the guitar and starting chording for my Dad when he played the fiddle and the mouth organ. I had started taking accordion lessons with the Royal Conservatory of Music as well. I wanted to take piano lessons but one had to start with accordion first and four years later I switched to the piano. All of these are creative spaces to hide and get lost in the world of oneself. I have outlets in my life but some are not so lucky.

Around this time I started to make sure I stayed away from terrible people as much as I could. You start to manoeuver jockey and position so you are not alone with certain people. You become smarter at trying to mitigate the risk on you. You hide a lot both physically and mentally so you are not found. If you make yourself scarce or alone no one can harm you. Let us call it survival 101 of the young. No one should have to grow up that way. It will take our collective communities at large to be cognitive and aware of this in order to better help the young people in our community more.

All are not aware in my circle and now I have the courage and strength to make them more aware. The goal so they may be able to spot warning signs in the future and be able to first spot hurt and pain and then help to stop it. Now that I know better now that I have more tools in my tool kit and more confidence I look forward to managing this with grace and dignity and with full on love. With no hostility and zero pity I embrace this simply to bring awareness and to help others feel comfortable to out their stories of abuse in hopes of more healing.

I have come to fully realize I am not angry anymore for their actions. I am sad to think about what happened to these people during their formative years that they think these actions are okay. I wonder what they have endured in their lives. Many people that are damaged are still running from themselves today.

I work diligently on forgiving that little girl the young lady the woman that did not speak up. I forgive me for not telling someone earlier or asking for help. I forgive those people for not seeing or noticing along the way or asking why? I do forgive and politely hold my ground I am just one person with a big heart and a want to stop all pain. Whether we like it or not we are responsible for our actions and all actions do have consequences today, tomorrow and always. Whether we run or not at some point we face the music. It is best to confront now so we may do the liberty dance for the rest of our days. Trust me I have started this dance and it feels wonderful. Heck what is the alternative more of the same forever? Not likely now that you are becoming aware.

YOUNG ADULT

CONFUSED

With the two oldest already out of the house and married in 1972 and another sibling married in 1975 there was more disposable income. My younger cousin had started taking dance because of one of her friends and she got me started. I think she asked my parents if I could join. I am glad she did. It was magical. It gave me another chance to escape. I did not realize that then. But to express one's self with body and tell a story is such a great form of expression and release. I did not have the right body for a ballerina but I could emote and express very well. It was an outlet I loved and another clue to my true identity yet to be fully understood. The stage offered an opportunity to escape in a crowd and a fantasy.

Growing up I did not realize I avoided confrontations about something or someone or anything. I did not clue in that I should have dealt with things instead of saying nothing about what was going on and how I was feeling. I really did not understand what was going on. How could anyone make sense of that? More education at all levels and awareness would mean the warning signs are visible faster. Being able to spot the pain faster is very important to correcting the low self-esteem and confidence issues of our young.

In my mind I was very spoiled compared to my brother and sisters. Or it could have been as a parent after your first child the second is easier you know what to expect. I can imagine after me the fifth child my Mom and Dad had pretty much seen it all and were a little more lenient. We all get more comfortable as parents the more children we have as was in my case as well. We had seen it once before so for our second child it was not so foreign. We were older parents as well which contributed to level of patience I am sure and my Mom and Dad were older parents too. In my own eyes I feel I got away with a lot. There were some instances I would like to take back in my life such as when my Mom would have to walk to work because as a teenager I had the car. Or I would take the car to University and instead of parking where we were allowed where it was far to walk to school I would park close and get a parking ticket everyday instead. I do not know how long it took but a sheriff did show up at our door for my Dad because I had given his license plate over twenty five hundred dollars of parking tickets. It was pay the Sheriff or he was taking my Dad. My Dad got his cheque book out. Of course I stopped parking close. I cannot remember for the life of me any hard punishment. Was this lashing out because I was angry with my parents for not helping me or asking me what was going on as I was growing up?

It took me until my twenties to come back to my parents and apologize for all these acts. My Mom was thankful that I had even acknowledged this. She said that was all she ever wanted. I think there was an element of spoiled and selfish but I also think it was my way of acting out for no one noticing my pain.

With my love of dance and performing I would translate this into an opportunity to have my own Ballet and Modern Jazz School of Dance. I studied at a local dance school in our town. As we got older and with proper dance accreditation the owner would set up a satellite school in an outlying area that did not have any dance programs. I studied the Cecchetti style of ballet and earned my elementary ballet, level five jazz my Associate Membership from Canadian Dance Teachers Association as well as my Teaching Certificate in ballet and jazz from Dance Teachers Club of Boston. I was the first one to be given a satellite school and it was my side hustle job during University. I had one hundred and twenty students and we would manage this over one evening of classes and all day Saturday classes in Cassleman and Embrun two small towns outside of Ottawa. I was attending full time University I had a teaching gig I had my own three or four dance classes a week and I was a Rhythm Rider that had three three hour practices a week plus game day and booked appearances. Keep busy keep safe was the mantra. To some looking in from the outside it may have looked different to them. Maybe it looked like strong or confident. I can put up a brave front. Fake it until you make it but in the long run that never works.

During my University years I had summer jobs with our Federal Government. Some included working for The Canadian Revenue Agency, The Department of National Defence, and Health and Welfare. I worked very hard and was very quiet. It was a good combination for an office environment and at the end of each summer I was asked to stay. I would politely decline and return to University. After my third year of University I set up an office for twenty people. That included everything from material management to telephone lines all while managing the

LOST VOICE

Executive Assistant functions for a Special Assistant to a Deputy Minister of the Canada Revenue Agency also known as the CRA. I still have the gold chain I was given as a parting gift after working four months that summer.

I could not toot my own horn at all but my hard work and perseverance showed and that is what people noticed. One's actions speak louder than words and they always will. I have never asked for a raise in any of the jobs I have had in my life. The raises or the opportunities were offered to me for my hard work dedication action and results. It is okay to ask for a raise do not get me wrong who does not like to be recognized.

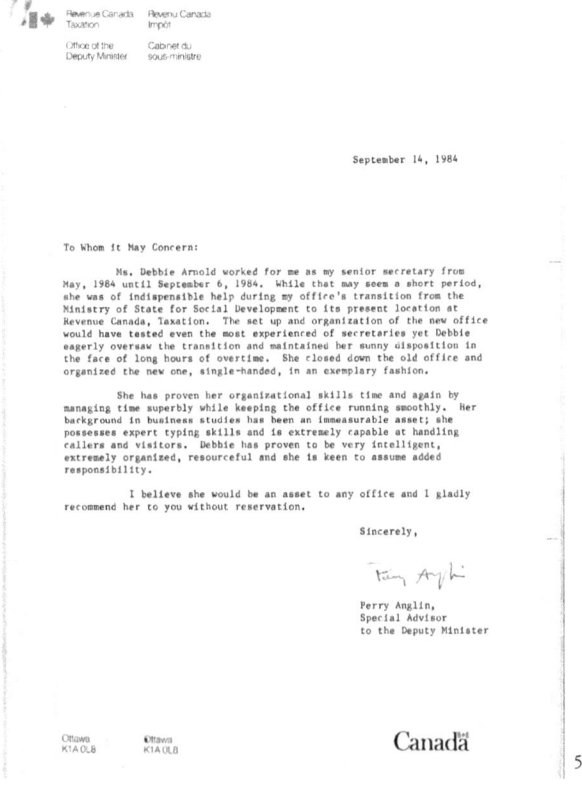

Many people have it worse. Many families are not a cohesive unit of love. Many are a hot mess waiting to explode. There are so many faces of abuse some include: abandonment, sexual, physical, mental, emotional and verbal. They are just some of the forms of maltreatment. I have experienced many of them. So many other stories and journeys of pain I know of which are so sad too. It should not sting this much to move forward in life yet for many it does. I know of peoples who are adopted in life but I do not know of many who are adopted suffer through sexual or physical abuse and then as a young teenager get abandoned again. I know of several in my life who suffer from this. How that must make one feel and how would one go forward from there? I know of a young girl where her parents are split up and neither Mom nor Dad wanted her and both told her same to her face she is in her mid-twenties. How does a young one make sense out of that? It is easy to see where the struggles for some adults come from once you are in the know.

That one experience where you are outed out in public and so embarrassed and ridiculed or someone says to you "that is a stupid idea." But these are words and put downs you hear every day. You can't do that, that is stupid who do you think you are? And we make the mistake of taking their word they must know. But truly they are barking back their fears on us to see how we would handle their anxieties and stress. This is another sign of low self-esteem on their end not yours or mine. My Mom and many others say "ye who yells the loudest has the most to hide" or something along those lines. I was not confident enough in myself to say "I do not care what you think I am pursuing my true calling in life" but I am confident enough now though. Usually at this point the dream or vision dies on the vine.

I use to say I am late bloomer but really I am just where I am supposed to be.

One incident is burned in my mind as young person we were in the school yard around where I lived. I was with a friend and we had the tennis rackets and balls. My friend did not have the confidence to swing that racket in public. They had never played tennis before and did not want to look stupid. Sounds silly doesn't it? But there was no one around. A car here and there driving by but they could not envision themselves running for the ball and making the swing without looking stupid or being ridiculed so they just did not try. This type of behaviour for this friend did not start happening that day over at the school yard. This behaviour was instilled with so much fear and not being loved in their family that they could not try anything in life. Can you imagine what they missed out on or are still missing out on in life? They endured a lot of mistreatment and suffering. I am sending love, strength and courage to all the wounded who need it most and need it now. The world needs your talents. It needs all of us and our unique ideas too.

During the years I was hanging out and sleeping over at my friends more than living at home I bumped into a lot of different people. For a while I hung with the older crowd of that house. Hanging out just making bad choices like working on gathering your money collectively in the group to purchase party favours. Deciding where we would hang out. We could go to the corner store with a note saying my Moms in the shower we are here to pick her up six beers and as minors we were sold that beer. It was not hard to get into trouble and being the youngest it was pretty easy to not be missed. By this time the three older siblings were well out of the house and starting families of their own. I hung at my friends from grade seven and eight through Community College called Cegep in Quebec and on into my first year University. I finally became someone's girlfriend at fourteen and we went out for the next seven years. We met at my friend's house where I slept over all the time. It took two years on my part to be successful in getting this boy as my boyfriend. He was two years older and I was too young for a long time.

My identity for the next seven years was his identity. I went from little sister to someone's boyfriend. We hung with his friends from his group. It crossed over a bit to my friend where I slept over so much because the older sibling and their friends and my boyfriend were buddies. So I got to tag along because of who I was going out with. I was never the lively outspoken one of the group but just a part of the group. Like on the fringe of the group you would call it. I certainly did not call the shots or decide what or where the group would go or what they would do. Five years into the relationship I broke it off. I felt like maybe I had grown up with this boy that we were more like brother and sister and maybe we should consider other people in our lives. I crushed him and we got back together three weeks later. We got engaged after the break up and then two years later he did same to me for the same reasons and broke off with me. I was depressed bewildered clueless and in a daze for close to a year. I cried a lot more than I normally did do. Sometimes emotions are a roller coaster. This was an exceptionally rough period for me.

Okay so maybe that relationship was more like brother and sister but the loss still stung. My grade point dropped and I quit a couple of classes at the University. I curled up in the fetal position a lot. I lost the group of friends in the circle of my life. I was no longer anyone not even someone's girlfriend. Yes I had a lot of things to do and I had a lot of acquaintances and I could have probably forged stronger bonds with friends but I was not aware that I was not doing that. There was a lot of alone time to think and reflect as best a messed up person can. I was coming up to finishing my Bachelor of Commerce. I realized I liked economics and that I also liked learning about the social impact on people, places and things. I guess stemming from what I had seen and experienced through my life first hand equality and inclusion were big for me then and still are today.

Home alone one Friday night I called Kids Help Phone. Ah you think because I broke up with someone I went out with for seven years right? Wrong. I called Kids Help Phone distraught that my fellow man would not help my fellow man. For me man is man, woman and child. I talked with Kids Help Phone for thirty minutes. They did not know what to do with me. They had never had a call like that before. I was encouraged to work with charities.

If the pieces of the messy puzzle called my life could have been assembled or I had some direction earlier on how best to assemble the pieces I am sure the struggle that did ensue would not have been for so long. The where with all and fortitude to have a clue of what I was attempting to piece together to make sense of my jumbled life is pretty freaking amazing if you ask me. Seriously though how naïve was I to not let someone into my world if only for a glimpse. I am thankful that I eventually did. And I remind myself daily beating myself up for not getting here sooner will only eat me up and give me health issues no quality of life and no peace of mind. So I will not go there.

During this breakup even in my darkest times I imagined in my head where the light is and things are safe my plan for world peace. If I was going back for a Master's Degree it would be in Social Economics and my thesis would be that I could find and ask everyone in the world what their utopia was what would make them happy for the rest of their lives? I would prove that we have enough to fulfil the desires and this was in the early eighties. Where my life events depression and bewilderment took my mind and how I made sense of it all is remarkable. In first creation I still managed to lay out a plan in my head. It is all I had that was pure and not sullied. I am determined to see this to fruition in my lifetime. I have created it so many times in my head I can see my version of world peace so clearly.

With my dance experience I thought about trying out for the Ottawa Rough Rider cheerleading team. More like my mind's eye was set to where else can I run away to hide and not be seen. I was successful in 1980 and during my second year under the choreography of Donna Staub a Philadelphia Eagle Cheerleader herself and as one of her leaders on and off the field we attended the Grey Cup at the Olympic Stadium in Montreal in 1981. The Ottawa Rough Riders with Jordan Case and Tony Gabriel against the Edmonton Eskimos what a great experience. Out of my five years on this fantastic team I earned the right to be an Assistant Captain for one season and Captain for two seasons. What an honour, privilege and thrill this was. It was not to be taken lightly. Unfortunately we were not successful in our Grey Cup attempt in 1981. Apart from Donna for a while but today reconnected and blessed for her guidance in my life as a mentor and divine spiritual leader but mostly as a beautiful friend. Her light and love shine bright for the world to see. Everyone needs light on their side.

Many of the girls that were on the team during this time still see each other regularly today. The current Ottawa Redblacks invite us Alumni Cheerleaders back once a year to do a pregame dance with the current Redblacks Dance and Cheer Team. It is great to keep in touch with the girls that we danced and cheered with over thirty years ago. The Redblacks sisterhood is an amazing atmosphere. These are positive and empowered women and men. It is nice to have the chance to reconnect once a year. This coming August will be my third year back as an Alumni.

I also partook in modelling classes and did a few local television commercials. Modelling was a place for people to look at me and for me to feel wanted but safe and away from being talked to or anyone expecting anything from me at the same time.

Time does heal that is true and about eight months later I would be in my second relationship. We were both taking a Bachelor of Commerce and our majors were finance with a minor in marketing. We were in most of the same classes. We would end up in the same study groups. Instead of being x's girlfriend I was now y's girlfriend but at least I had some identity. Same but different you know? Our time together was limited to the circle of friends from University.

Often family events would come up in this new relationship such as going out on the lake sailing. He would say things like "it is just for family and I hope you understand." Not just a couple of times but any time a family event came up. He was never interested either to meet my family. I could not follow the dots the path or the reasoning then. He came from a family of influence from the financial world. They were from the Toronto area. My boyfriend was in Ottawa attending school and stayed during the summer months for work. The family had a membership at the Glen Abbey Golf Course I certainly never attended.

Simply put I was not adequate enough nor was I worthy enough to meet his family. I was the unknown questionable girl from the other side of the river. I was second class. If I knew then what I know now seems to be the story of my life. Do not let it be yours too.

Our athleticism and sense of adventure connected me to my next relationship. I bumped into him the first time in the fall one year. He lived with my friend and some other people that they both knew. I went to visit my friend and a whole group were going out to a bar. I joined them and we all streamed out of the house and walked downtown to a club that was playing live blues music. I danced with one of my next relationships friends that evening. And that was that.

It was a full year later I was with another friend and we were in a line up to get into Stoney Mondays a popular night club at the time. The guy I met a year ago at my friends poured out the side door of the night club for a cigarette with one of his buddies. He recognized me in the lineup with my friend and said "hey I can get you guys in here come on this way". So my friend and I snuck in the side door.

He was there with his football team. The night club was a team sponsor. He was a good line backer. We made a bet that night. I bet that he could not sit on the floor extend his legs and touch his head to his knees. If he did I would buy dinner and if he did not he would buy me dinner. He won and I bought dinner this was in October that year.

I was a cheerleader with the Ottawa Rough Riders of the Canadian Football League (CFL). He played football one level under the professionals. It was love at first site. It was a beautiful fall with all the trees turning colors. We could go for walks around Ottawa just holding hands. We were fond of quiet stops at neighbourhood outdoor cafés. Ottawa had and still does have many trendy vibrant spots and streets. Bank Street, Elgin Street and The By-Ward Market are still some of the most happening places in our Nations' Capital, along with TD Place on Bank Street where my beloved Redblacks play and The Canadian Tire Center where I adore it when the mighty Maple Leafs trounce those Senators. We would frequent one bar in particular the kind of vibrant bar and grill with great live bands and a great patio that spilled out onto the Bank Street sidewalk. I am not sure if it is still there today?

We were both active people and liked adventure and still do today. It did not make a difference what we were doing a walk a nice quiet dinner or watching some television we hang out well together. Depending on the season we could skate the seven kilometer Rideau Canal or ski at one of the hills in the Outaouais Valley or swim cottage or camp with friends. I actually pushed him one way on the Rideau Canal from start to finish as he was bent over with hands on knees just for the heck of it for something to do.

We could walk and not say anything but say everything. Shortly into the relationship I could see that I could spend the rest of my life with this person. I envisioned and I still do today his and her rockers at ninety two with lemonade on the front porch watching the world go by. You could see his acts of kindness even in the smallest things. It could be as simple as if he was getting himself a drink he would always ask if you wanted one and he still does today. I moved in with him before the snow came that year. His friends and my friend were moving out and it gave us a chance to move in together.

One of our many walks early on in our relationship was around the neighbourhood that I grew up in. He can say the most profound things at times. He understood that I had never had a voice growing up. He shared with me that it is okay that Debbie has a voice. That no one else has that voice. That really resonated with me. But I went overboard as one might say. From zero voice to slamming my idea thought or opinion right down your throat. You were going to listen to what I had to say one way or another.

Not pretty the opposite actually very ugly indeed. He, my friend and his friends tried to show me some examples or make me aware of my arrogant voice and for a while I wanted nothing to do with it. I was going to have my say. That did not work well at all I was too obnoxious. Not pretty. I clued in that I had to tone it down and basically reverted back to old Debbie. That new one only lasted not even a month. I had gone overboard.

After moving in we had gone to meet his parents in Toronto and we were just a couple of months into the relationship and he asked me to marry him. I said yes and an elopement was under way. We had just seen what a couple of weddings ended up like once the families were involved and we decided that was not what we wanted. We were married at the Justice of Peace in Ottawa and unbeknownst to us my Mom and sister were both around the corner having a coffee break while on a shopping trip. We rented witnesses from the Justice of Peace office as well. We honeymooned skiing Whiteface in Lake Placid. A couple of young twenty somethings ready to take on the world but would love be enough?

I did not realize throughout all my relationships this one included that I never had my own identity. I was someone's younger sister, girlfriend, wife or Mom. I was someone with a face no name and no voice. I was part of the group but without opinion. Just went along it was easier than the alternative confrontation or worse picked on or teased by the group. So nothing bothered me I did not offer my opinion or any of my ideas or thoughts on any subject. I kept most of my opinions to myself. I did not bother to stick up any more when I was insulted or picked on it was easier to just say nothing. Safe subjects in the circle are how is the weather, how is so and so, how was your day at work and what are you up to tomorrow? It really is not a way to go through life.

FOR BETTER OR WORSE

CHAOS

In everything there is the good, the bad and the ugly. Common sense tells you the good should far outweigh the bad and the ugly combined. If I am working towards that and making progress then life is good. But if you keep coming up short then something is just not right and in order to move on you have to manage, handle and confront.

The good has always outweighed the bad in my case. My senses told me something was not right early on but I felt there were zero options so I carried on. It would take a long time for my head and heart to catch up and to enact. There are always ways to hide to cover up to appear as other as a master of disguise. Fake it until you make it. It starts with a really great foundation makeup you put a smile on your face and you carry on like nothing happened. You sweep it all under the carpet. See no evil, hear no evil and speak no evil all of which is wrong and not the proper way to deal with any thing in life.

In for a penny in for a pound all those great vows and knowing that our great Divine never turns his back on anyone. How can mankind then turn their back? What gives me the right? How can I turn my back? What of the love I have and feel. What of the children being a good parent being a great role model managing a career that will support the family creating a legacy the relationship or what about you? The pressures and stresses of life are a lot to juggle. Wake up get on the merry go round and repeat this recipe for disaster. All compromised of a general sense of hurry up and go hustle and bustle keep up with the neighbours next door and on your street on the journey to nowhere of great destination just a journey of survival. You have to break the cycle. It took me a long time but it is the only way if you want to get to love of self. We live in a country where violence against someone is flat out wrong. There are boundaries that cannot be crossed. Everyone has rights as a Canadian Citizen. Why are we so afraid to act upon violence in the home? I have enacted and I can tell you respect and self-worth are not in the toilet anymore and I certainly do not want to be anywhere near that point again and I truly wish the same for everyone.

Of course if we never change the input we cannot expect a different outcome. Every so often a glimpse of what was possible would show itself enough to sustain that there is hope and that we must never give up. In my case I know there is enough to go on.

The sexual assaults from childhood were traded for mental, physical, verbal abuse and working through arresting someone in my life. I endured a lot in life by way of trauma and abuse. Terrible acts of indecency. Describing each detail of these triple digit events that occurred against me does not serve or bring any value? Graphically it paints a picture of indecent acts against people which is horrible to experience and live through. Any act of violence upon someone is heartbreaking and devastating. It is one too many acts. It does not need qualifying or quantifying for that is personal and unique to each of us to walk people through as we see fit or to let them in as we see fit. It will always remain about your healing not someone else's healing. I know now that suffering in silence was wrong.

Working up the corporate ladder came next. I would come home at the end of the work week so stressed out. I would get home and be sick literally throw up and go to bed. I would just push the envelope and burn the candles at both ends. Not smart enough to realize it was just a form of running away. I am also a perfectionist and I must be working towards something if not that makes me sick too. It is just who I am in life. A stress induced migraine until the being sick would release the tension.

I would work so long that when my body tells me enough is enough it needs to be horizontal. And only my body will tell me that I have had enough rest and I can get up without being sick. Sometimes that means sleep for forty hours. I was at work one morning in the gym exercising before work. I was alone it was six thirty a.m. I went down on the floor in the change room. I knew I was down for the count. I slept for about an hour. I could not get up. A lady came in the change room. I asked her to go up to the company I worked for and to please get one of the girls from my office. She did and a girl from my office came down and wanted to call an ambulance. I said "no I am just wiped out." I asked her to get my colleague when he came to the office so he could drive me to friends in town where I could sleep until my husband could come down from up north later that evening and pick me up to take me home. I woke up at nine p.m. in the City and he drove me home to bed where I slept another twenty four hours. High pressured job deadlines feeling bad when you cannot deliver the mail that is tied to a television or radio ad. When I see people working late and not appreciating life now I think to myself are they running away from an unhealthy home life like I have done in the past or is this really their passion and their drive. This happened for many years. Of course speaking with someone would have got the ball rolling faster and I realize now is the correct and only thing to do. I am not going to whip myself into frenzy over it. It is not something I can control so I will not waste any precious energy on it. I got there and that is all that matters.

I attended two separate women related stress courses that my work put me through. And I still remember two great things I learned. The first is why women wait until they are horizontally sick to do anything. Why we do not see that most times we are vertical and walking wounded. The second thing I learned is that we are never more elastic in life than what we are now. Once a break down occurs we will never be this elastic again. Take care of all of you.

Please find the courage to get to a safe place so you can begin your new life one without pain and hurt.

BROKEN AND WITHOUT A VOICE

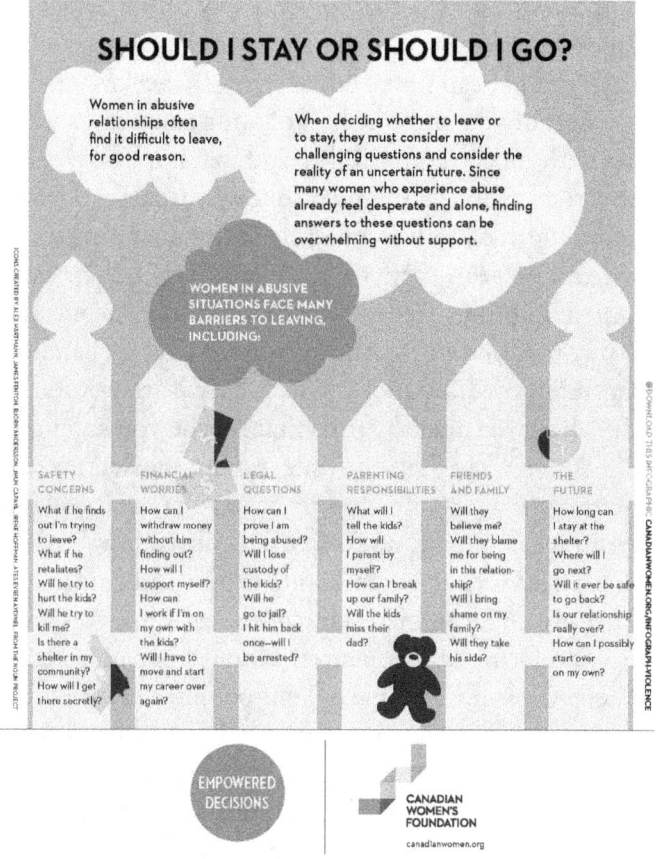

My Dad died when I was thirty six and after that life changing event I realized that you stressed over family and that nothing else matters. My clients could yell at me anyone could yell at me try and control me but none of these things were life or death. The sky would still be blue and I would still breathe. Hard lesson to learn when my Dad died but it sure puts it into perspective pretty darn fast what really matters in life. The crazy sayings like sweat the big stuff not the little stuff are extremely valid.

Children too help change your way of life or perspective in life or modify it. They are the true miracles of life. Something that can never be taken away they are made up of one half of you and one half of your partner. Parenting comes with much responsibility and making sure you leave a good road map for them to follow. Parenting is not to be taken lightly. How you handle and manage everything in life can be seen higher wider and deeper than can be imagined. I know I needed to finally talk to someone about agony in my life so my children would have a chance and a road map to which they could follow or refer too.

It is hard to come to terms that maybe you should talk to someone? Wow that must mean I am messed up right? You wrestle that around in your head to make it feel okay. Why do we wait so long to figure it out? How I made it work for me was I am a marketing expert and corporations and people come to me each day to learn how to market their product or service better. How to get more clients and keep the ones they have. So if people come to me the expert for marketing can I not go to someone who is an expert in life that can listen to my life plan? Absolutely I can and I am glad I took that step. They help to clear things up so the healing time is shortened. You can see the concerns a little more clearly. They can help you check and balance your life. They can share or recommend coping and managing skills. They help to identify the triggers and if there are any barriers still to come down. There are so many different types of support. Finding what resonates with you and what makes sense for you is what is most important. It is like the key to the city except it is the key to you. The important take away is open up and spill your guts with someone you trust or find someone a walk in clinic if it is all you have. If you are all alone they should be able to give you some guidance and direction. You need to find someone you can trust.

At this point I was doing it for the children not for me. The on-going awareness and education that ensued for the whole family is a measure that was instrumental in setting up a plan that helped everyone involved.

At plus three decades into the marriage if I could say it has been easy I would not be telling the truth. Most parts are like those that you only read about in fairy tales, but others not so much. Can I say that most of it has been good? Yes I can without hesitation or reservation. Do I think that throwing in the towel is the answer? No I do not in my case. Do I think where there is enough love, acceptance, ownership, awareness and on-going education where each other are in their journey of life there can be peace and harmony? Emphatically yes I do. Am I safe? Yes I am.

There is a long way to go. It is a journey on the way to a destination. Some parts will be a breeze and some will be a bit more challenging to work through. Currently I am a bit stuck in ownership and accountability but nothing that cannot be overcome. For me I will concentrate on accountability in counselling. I cannot make the whole world accountable in one day. I am not accountable for actions of others. I can point them out and try to show them the way of the light and the Universe. But they must make the changes in their life. We are ultimately all accountable for our actions whether we verbalize the ownership or not.

The love runs deep and where there is a will there is a way. But being safe is one of the basic needs of life as in Maslow's hierarchy of needs and everyone must have these basic needs covered or there is no going forward.

Triggered by stresses of life people usually pull on their past experiences almost by instinct. This requires keeping up on all coping mechanisms that are available to ensure one is armed with knowing the trigger points. Knowing the coping skills that are necessary to work through things openly and avoid pulling the wrong experience from the back pocket. For example you use to smoke and you have not had a cigarette for five years but you are in a most stressful situation and you start to smoke again. People resort to what is comfortable and what is known. It is torment to dig for answers during times of stress. But unless you dig there is no possibility of going forward for you are stuck in this place of torture forever.

I am sincere with my wish for all to be able to manage and confront things that life throws us. To handle both the good and the bad in a respectful and reasonable way is the direction we want to aim towards. We all know that it is the right way and we all know that deep down inside. As well for me personally I wish to leave a road map for future generations to follow. Getting to an expert that can help guide you through your journey is also helpful. At the forefront forever is love of self.

Up until 2012 I compromised Debbie my whole life. Then things started happening and the pieces started coming together with more clarity, certainty and confidence. The children went off to school and had moved out of the house. Time opens up. You have more time to reconnect to the things that are important in your life or your journey of well-being simply begins in earnest. There was more time to have conversation with your significant other and to return to the days of walks playing guitars and enjoying life together. I did not know at the time exactly what I was preparing for but I knew I needed to be of strong body mind and soul for the unknown that lay ahead.

I am blessed. I had a lot to begin with. My Mother our Lord and a belief in myself that I knew there was good inside me. I always had at least three people with me at any given time if no one else. I had me myself and I. I had that inside voice in my head and it was a strong voice full of light and love. I tried hard not listen to all those ugly outside voices I heard every single day of my life. These three people are very powerful and are all I needed. I realize even more now that it is all we ever need along with guidance, affirmation and acceptance from whatever life force guides you and your life. Thank you to the Universe for affirmation in my life path and journey forward in full regalia and with full voice. In borrowed words of a friend woot woot! Your journey begins with love of you and so we begin together.

For me the choice is to stay and continue to work on growing and healing together. That may not always be for everyone and that is okay. The important take away is that the choice is yours to make and no one else's. It begins with safety first. Then you have to take care of you and it is not being selfish. It means you have enough respect of self to be safe and to love self. There is no confusion about hurt and pain. They are not acceptable in our society. From the love side there are many emotions and feelings running through one's head for both sides of that coin. This is a really good point in your life to reach out and talk this through with someone. It is okay to get some help and talk out what makes sense for you. Safety will always be paramount and in this chapter there is an *Infographic* from Canadian Women's Foundation.[6] It outlines practical tips to make sure your safety is covered. A checklist to make sure you are prepared to leave with everything thought out and covered. To remember you need first to get to safety. Connect with me at DebbieMajor.ca for other tips to gain the courage and strength to manage the barriers that are holding you back.

CARNAGE LEFT
EFFECT

Until you are on the other side you never really understand the full impact or lasting effect of what was taken from you as a child. The other side or arriving refers to the place one is with the inevitable admission Houston we have a problem.

But until then I did not realize the full significance it had on me and later the control it had on my life, my choices and decisions. Definitely there was an effect or aftermath. The darkness had influenced everything in my life until this moment.

I partook in a lot of things in and around the community after the trip to the Doctor wherein he told my Mom to keep me busy. I went to Sunday school and partook in all the Church activities. Sleigh rides, sugar bush visits, Sunday school picnics, plays, bible class, Canadian Girls in Training , brownies, and playing with the neighbourhood kids are a few. We had lots of nature hills, valleys, swimming ponds and quarries to explore and keep us busy too. We were allowed to stay out until the street lights came on. Our family did a lot together as well such as camping, sport events, sing songs and family gatherings all such fun and great times and they continue today. I am blessed to come from a loving house. That fact alone with the great influence of my Mom and the message I heard at church each week I can honestly say is what kept me from giving up on myself. I knew deep down I was unique just as you all are. I was given un-killable un-stoppable spirit drive grit tenacity and staying power. I just did not know or fully understand how it all fit together and certainly did not have the confidence and strength to speak up so I just suffered in silence. Like many of you do too.

I remember letting my older brother know I felt like I did not belong in my family. I am sure many young people feel this way. I was trying to let him know of the agony I was carrying. We were in my Mom and Dad's room in front of their large double panel mirrored closet. It was a simple room a double bed two night tables one lady's and one man's chest of drawers and my Mom's makeup table. Everything was made out of beautiful oak wood except for the makeup table. The house was twelve hundred square feet with three bedrooms and one bathroom. Mom and Dad took the second biggest bedroom and left the big room for us three girls to share. It would have been around this time my older brother was married and his visit was most likely for Sunday family supper. My brothers shared the smallest room before one was married and later it would be Mom's sewing room and then Dad's room when he snored too much for Mom. I think I was about twelve. I could not get out why I was so sad I guess. I could not connect the dots for my brother. He would have been around twenty seven. He hugged me and told me sure I belonged. I was not able to talk to my parents they were in their forties they would not understand or so I thought. I just knew I should not have a sick tummy my whole life. My poor brother he was not equipped to manage or let alone even know what I was trying to get out.

The formative years are just that. They shape and mold you and become part of your subconscious. Mine were messed up. I realize now that a lot of kids formative years are messed up. I wanted to tell people as a kid how it stung but I could not confront them I was too scared. The lack of confidence is ingrained from the beginning. Someone who has confidence finds this hard to understand maybe even conceive. Those who have full love of self are very blessed. They should be thankful and rejoice. They are in a great place to continue to share their passion, love and happiness where ever they go and whatever they do. Perhaps they take their confidence as a given. Or perhaps they feel everyone comes preloaded with confidence already. But it is taken from many or kept from many in life for many reasons. It is however possible to love all of you and gain confidence. You are a growing living thing and are a dynamic changing human being. Only you have your uniqueness and no one else does. DNA from science would support this unique theory as well. It is absolutely breath taking to see and feel someone who is with full confidence and full love of self. You too can get there.

Those without love, encouragement, belief, love of self or confidence are overwhelmed whether out of pure necessity or other. They do not have the luxury to think about self or drive. It is about manage, exist and survive. The path or the swath of carnage left in life is a path that is wide deep dark and destructive. It touches and has effect on every aspect of life from this unwanted eventful day forward. Ability to see and think clearly and make reasonable decisions and control journey and destination is not possible. Ability to reach full potential is but a distant memory or an unreachable dream and only for those who are truly worthy. In quiet unison we suffer. There are no boundaries or borders to the suffering on one's soul just a vicious cycle – loop to nowhere except agony and defeat. It was not until recently I stopped running took stock realized the gifts inside gained confidence and said I am good. I am of use I do belong I have reason for being and drive. Watch me grow and learn. Just watch me.

    I can honestly say other than when I was performing I was a wall flower. I would sit on the sidelines of life and watch. I would not speak. Dying to be in the activities going on knowing I could but never having the courage. Talent shows at school I would want to try out but fear would hold me back. I saw our high school band and they had singers. I wanted to be part of the band so badly. I knew I could sing like the other girls in the band but I could not get up enough confidence to try out. The list goes on and on. Tryouts for dance solos try outs for cheer solos not a chance not happening here. Having to wait to be picked for a sports team or a project to be worked on in class made me so sad and sick. I was one of the last to be picked always. I was too shy to be wrong in class or singled out. To insecure to be laughed at even more scared to be ridiculed or picked on so I would rather not say anything. I was so worried about being watched or spotted it was hard to ever concentrate on what was being said in class. I usually missed whatever was being said so of course I could never answer well when I was called upon. Standing up with all eyes upon you, your head and your thoughts are empty other than you feel fear and you just want them to stop looking at you. The feeling of mortification sets in.

    Part of the effect of abuse and trauma is it limits what you try for in life. Many promotions I would not consider because I knew I would not get them so why even bother. Or so I thought. But to not bother is a waste to you your legacy and to the greater world and mankind. For me mankind is man, women and child. It is pure golden on the other side of dark it is alive and we definitely all deserve to be truly alive.

    I felt humiliated and embarrassed as a child in public school in high school and most of my life. I kept wondering why or trying to answer it fully but I did that in silence. Literally it shuts you down. It shuts voice, self, body, mind, feeling, emotions and soul down. It eats you alive bit by bit. It strips you naked leaves you vulnerable and exposed. It leaves you more susceptible to being bullied because they smell your weakness. They somehow know you do not or will not stand up. You might as well stomp on me. I was a door mat after all. However I no longer let people wipe their ugly off on me. None of us should wear other people's ugly.

    It is like this empty tunnel even at a young age with nowhere to turn and no end in sight. Who do you tell? What do you tell? Maybe you have already told a bit and now you have to deal with family humiliation and shunning even if the people believe you. I can read sad in many eyes and I can pick out sad eyes in any crowd. I cannot be the only one to see this sorrow in people. Eyes truly are the windows of our soul. A starting point to bringing awareness and positive self-image can be found at DebbieMajor.ca

BROKEN AND WITHOUT A VOICE

Grade Nine Age Fourteen[7]

High School Graduation Grade Eleven Age Sixteen[8]

There are many great online sites to help understand the effect on adults who have survived childhood trauma and abuse. Just to read and become comfortable with and realize that we may have a lot of these symptoms. Some symptoms we may have managed better than others. Even to understand the full breath of what is deemed abuse is very revealing and pulls at my heart. No person on earth should suffer with this ache. By definition abuse is cruel and violent treatment of a person or animal.

Part of the plan would be to develop the road map to health and liberty that is unique to you and your situation. I found the information at centrefortherapy.ca[9] very helpful. But there are many such sites to begin with as well as reaching out and getting to that expert who can really help. Types of abuse are different for each individual person. This list is no way exhaustive but can include:

- Verbal
- Sexual
- Physical
- Mental
- Abandonment
- Not the chosen child of the family
- Loneliness
- Depression
- Substance abuse
- Family shunning
- Family exclusions
- A life changing event
- Any other blockers that bring misery, suffering and inaction

We bring our cars to a garage to get fixed and we bring our broken bones to a Doctor to mend. It is now time to bring our broken self to a professional so we can mend. It is the biggest part of you. We all want and strive to be our best to be one hundred percent and not running at a mere fraction of what we could be. I cannot impress enough we all have value within.

The bad acts shut you down. Once or twice a week something serious would happen. Today you will be going along in life and an image will pop into your head. A memory well repressed and it comes to light. Talk about taking you back to the dark deep tunnel of torture for mind body and soul. Of late I have come to realize I repressed a lot of events. This is new for me. It is okay to morph and grow in our journey. Each day as we learn more our actions and thinking should also change based on that new acquired knowledge. We are never stagnant for long nor should we want to be. Someone close to me taught me this recently and I accept that I was wrong to think I did not repress any events. However I still do not think remembering each incident is helpful to healing and moving on either if you have identified your root pain. Dissecting each act or trying to remember them all for me personally serves no purpose. They were bad and why should I waste any more of my precious energy on those disgusting acts. I should translate that energy into something positive or it is a waste and so should you.

By natural occurrence when I have a flash back because something has triggered a memory I do not stop that event or feelings from flowing through me. There is usually a new learn a step or a piece to the puzzle you have been waiting for. If the hurt is so repressed getting to professional help can only assist you. You need to get to the root of it. To identify your pain or hurt and then what is the healing path for you. I share my root pain and blockers to make a map for you to follow. The goal is that you leave the agony behind you where it deserves to be. Take the learnings from the hurt leave the hardship and go on to the new you and the new beginnings so deserving.

I know we have value. I am of value so I use those hurts to be stronger and more aware of my true passion and calling. We need to collectively spread the word no more abuse embrace all of you do and be who you were intended to be.

We should not hold a grudge and we should forgive. What would be the benefit to us if we just held onto the grudge? There is absolutely no benefit. I am not missing a large gap or piece of who I am. To spend time in anger or darkness does not seem right either. Today I work on anger towards those who will not be accountable for their life. It is wrong to hold onto any kind of anger. I need to completely let that go for I cannot worry over something I have no direct control over such as someone else's actions. I also need to forgive myself completely for not stepping forward sooner. I was scared but I am not frightened any more.

Truthfully my goal is to show everyone how beautiful they are. And those people who are hurt and lost shower them with a stream of continual love and kindness so they realize they have special gifts too. I work diligently on this in therapy. I just need to flip the talk track in my head to be more in the other person's shoes and to understand where they come from. I believe then we are in a better position to help others. In its purest essence love and kindness is in us to give freely. The ability to help others to help people stop the hurt and love thy self is in all of us.

Each week crap happens and as a young child in the formative years you carry on as best you can. You do not join groups at recess in the playground and you stand by yourself with maybe another child who also gets picked on in school. You let kids call you names bad names and you stand in shame and take it. You cry inside and wonder why they hate you. You are seven years old. You think being an exhibitionist at seven on someone's front lawn or anywhere is what all kids do is it not? You get to be picked last for all the stuff going on at school or socially or better yet you do not get picked at all. I just remember feeling sick all the time. Then the crap still happens but now you are an adult.

So many times in class at school you just want to open up your desk and crawl in. Too embarrassed to answer a question I may be wrong and ridiculed. I had had enough public shaming I did not need to go looking for more that is for sure. The feeling of value just takes a nose dive and you are too young to even know what is going on. Unfortunately for many the stigma, dirt and stink stay for life because we do not realize it is not normal. But I know now that "that" is anything but normal.

I felt so dirty so ashamed. Some days I still feel soiled and no matter how many times you shower you cannot get the stink off. Then I remember that is not the aroma of my heart and soul no sir not a chance. I repeat to myself I am done. I am finished with hammering me anymore. When I got a little older and something bad would happen I would ask myself is that going to be the moment or event that takes me down? Is this the moment that will define me and finally kill my spirit my perseverance and my existence? No it would not be. No one but me was going to define me. I have not crossed something in my life yet that has defined me or killed my spirit. I am like that webble toy I can wobble but I will not fall down. I am thankful I have that spirit within me. Some say I just got it. Others say I have it from the Universe and some say I received it from the Divine and I say all three combined.

Those horrible acts could not win over me. Deep down I knew that was not the answer. I knew it was not going to be what won for good in my life. The attitude was it could define me or I could define it. It does not get easier as a teenager. The choices show themselves mostly in who you hang around with your aspirations and the kind of trouble you are getting into.

I am good I am great but one does wonder how much quicker one could have arrived had one not had to deal with all of this. A part of me thinks yes for sure I have experienced loss of earnings. Definitely the power to earn has been affected because of what I have been through. But that would be dwelling on the past not forgiving and not thinking of the great that we have or the greatness that is ahead. Instead spending our time concentrating on the dreary that is behind. That which sucks all our energy and ultimately our being therefore we must learn to let it go. We should also leave behind the: should have, could have and would have syndrome. It holds no purpose either. These negative items only hold you back for longer in getting to the richness of you and your true being. I am sorry *glorious readers* the world owes us nothing. It is there to guide and show the way when you wake up to beautiful you.

I struggled with family exclusions and being shunned. I think that is because of my sensitivity to excluding anyone. Left out and ignored. Do people understand what it feels like to be excluded in family or in anything in life? It means that someone has a list of names. They are going down that list and in their mind they are thinking of the people on the list. So they have to say the name out loud or in their head and then say yes or no. So they would get to my name and say no. This is family. Maybe it does not sound like a lot but a dozen or so milestone family events I was excluded from. My family was excluded from. Wedding showers, weddings and baby showers come to mind. We would get many times we wanted to but you understand we cannot. I am sorry family I do not understand we cannot. I had to explain that to my children they would ask why we were never invited. I always gave the truth when the children asked with an age appropriate answer. I received great advice from my sister who taught grade four. When children ask a question they deserve an answer. I have never forgotten that great message from my sister.

I try not to dwell but even today on a bad day it stings. Out of all the family not once did anyone in my circle ever stand in solidarity with me and say I am not going this time if you are not including all the family. No one ever did. Just the feeling of second class all the way baby. Not good enough. There is a lot about the people who harmed me that my family does not know about. To this day I do not know quite how that conversation will go but I do know it will go without malice or harm. For the purpose that generations current or future will not suffer unnecessarily like I did.

Ones most vulnerable secret or hurt is the best gift of healing you can pass on or leave as a legacy for the future, for family, generations to come, friends, community, city, province, country and world. It would be a shame to keep it cloaked in darkness when it may even help just one gather the courage and strength to finally stand free of hurt and openly sing ones praises. To rejoice of the new freedom of knowing who you are and finally okay to show it.

My voice today looks much different than my broken voice growing up.

I struggled most of my working career with having to facilitate work relations with people of not the greatest integrity ethics or morals. I struggled with this with many businesses. I reviewed where possible to remove myself from the questionable areas or to adjust my involvement. Today I am able to share whether within an association or within the work environment what I support and do not feel comfortable to support. I am able to do so in a professional diplomatic way. My decorum was not always so proper. There were times I was very unprofessional in meetings by putting people on the hot seat which is exactly how they made me feel. But two wrongs never make a right. I know better. So again I adjust the talk track in my head and I revert to my actions filled with kindness as that is a far better way to make an impact in life. It is a far better way to help people and businesses. With some I may not have the same relationship again or I may not have the relationship at all. Many employers and people play games of manipulation why I will never know. Again I would like to ask people who play manipulative games why they have to do that and find out where their torment outrage or suffering comes from or came from. Now I remember always to ask why? I am convinced that most times when we ask why we would find out that people come from growing up in perhaps not a good environment. Perhaps not having great role models or it could be many other things as well. Trying to find out why is always good. It never excuses the bad actions that people do but when you know why they do the bad actions it does help to understand both them and the situation better.

    With anger spite revenge the struggle within me took me to hell and back on more than a few times in my life. It took me for over three decades over thirty years of my life through a spin cycle of dreary ugly empty and alone up for air and back again. Mad like no tomorrow filled with rage. I wanted to take out a five thousand dollar full page ad in the hometown local newspaper to make sure everyone knew everything about the people who crippled me and spoiled me. Today I wonder about other children who are wounded and victims from abuse and how life has been for them.

I am where I am supposed to be with all the experiences I am to have for the next new part of the journey of my life. I do appreciate that I may have been able to get here sooner. If not for the incidents of heartache and sorrow throughout my life but it no longer holds me back or keeps me captive. They actually empower me to share as it is time we took better care of ourselves the world and everyone in it.

CHOICES MADE

IMPACT

You know how your gut tells you things are not right but your head tells you something else. Whatever it takes for you to think the torture is alright you fake yourself into thinking it will get better. So you just become numb to it. Your level of what normal looks like is way out of line.

All of this has an overwhelming impact on you. The friends you choose. The boyfriends you choose. How you act at social functions. The programs you choose to go into for school and higher learning. Your work decisions, who you hang out with and what you aspire too or dream of are just a few of the things that are impacted.

Some of those wrong or bad decisions has impact on being, capacity, merit, value, loss of potential, loss of freedom, loss of living, loss of income, loss of dignity and loss of self-respect to name a few. You can shrivel up and die or choose to come alive. I choose to shine and come alive and stand for love of self and for respect of self.

I should have pursued the arts. But I did not have enough confidence. My father said serious job only. I hear those words still today. I did not have a ballerina's body. I did try out for Les Grands Ballet Canadiens, The Royal Winnipeg Ballet and The National Ballet of Canada. How great is it that I got to take my audition at 5 pm one evening with Prima Ballerina Karen Kane of the National Ballet of Canada. It was during the casts warm up at the National Art Center in Ottawa before their performance of the Nutcracker. To be just a practice barre away from the greatest Ballerina in my opinion was a thrill I shall not ever forget. I tried out for a few Modern and Jazz Dance Troupes in the Ottawa area as well. I was always told I have incredible feeling but never landed a spot. I did not have enough turn out. I have flat feet and therefore did not have a pretty pointed foot. My legs are not long enough meaning torso to leg ratio. Hey you cannot be good at everything we must remember to keep trying until the special gift you have fits and the magic is found.

My coach and choreographer from the Ottawa Rough Rider Rhythm Riders would have taken me under her wing and helped me dance my way around the world on cruise ships with one of the best North American Production Companies at the time like she did. I really did not realize I had this opportunity. I would not have been strong enough to do that though at that time. I wonder what my life would have been or where I would be but wondering will only serve me up a dish of bitterness and regret. If I had just spread my wings and tried but it was not my time then it is now though. Leave the regrets at the door.

Even with all that I had been through at my young age I knew there was something outstanding in me. My organizational skills would serve me well in life and preparation was a big key. I was born to help and lead at an early age. I could not do it with my voice but I could do it with my actions and work ethic. Actions therefore always speak louder than words and most times our words do not equate to our actions. The impact was I could not share what I had been through or I could not share or find a way to let people know I was noteworthy. So I said nothing instead and kept my dream of my world peace plan to myself.

Coming out of childhood with confidence not intact, paltriness and inadequateness is what my radar was set to look for. Set to look for what you believe you are worthy of. Nothing I say. It was so ingrained in me and in my very being. In this state your bar is not set to its full potential. You go looking for where you think you will be accepted. The sexual abuse made its way to physical, mental and verbal insults during this point in my life. It felt like a natural transgression what I was deserving of. My senses very in tune though. I always knew when not to say anymore for fear of severe repercussions. It was just easier to not voice an opinion and to revert to the sidelines of life. It was much safer. There was less discomfort and blight. I know and the Universe knows what is going on. That is good enough for me. When an event transpires there are so many emotions things running through my head. Rage and some of it directed to who just injured me. Most times I directed the fury at me for being stupid for allowing it and not being strong enough to manage it. Mostly I was angry for not respecting me enough to do anything about it. I knew there was a cost to all of it. My life my existence and my being were in jeopardy. Fear held me back but not anymore.

This thinking this behaviour has gone on my whole life. Choices for relationships career the people I hung out with and the list goes on and on and on. It is all tied to lack of love of self and feeling invaluable, unloved and unwanted. It is all I knew my whole life and no one in my circle was aware.

Your level of tolerance is way out of whack. Or your confidence and give a hoot factor meter are set at zero and you believe that to be one hundred percent where it should be. Garbage is what garbage does just like a comfy worn out slipper it fits well.

We are just about to have our first child. About three weeks out and an overwhelming feeling comes over me. What am I thinking I cannot have this baby! I am not a person who can be a Mom. I have nothing to give. I did not mean it I am not ready take it back. Another effect of living with trauma and abuse is the feeling of being inadequate. Not being enough is so ingrained in everything you do and touch or feel in life it is all you know inside and out.

Small town hospital no epidurals available and my general anesthetic emergency C section went well. I got to ask one hour after birth if I had a beautiful girl or boy and they said "a girl." She is as beautiful at twenty four now as she was then. This was 1992 and I stayed in the hospital for six nights and seven days. A stay this long was unheard of even in the nineties. My baby was dehydrated and not latching on properly. If I could have asked for help maybe I would not have given my daughter urethra crystals. Dry crystallised urine from being dehydrated. I would rather cry alone in the hospital where help was available because that is way better than putting on your big girl pants and asking someone for help? I think one night at four or five a.m. a beautiful nurse managing the evening shift was close enough to see my tears. She was warm enough to ask "what's wrong dear?" That is all it took I had a complete breakdown but within two minutes she helped me realize my daughter is not a china doll she will not break you have to push or with energy latch their mouths on. But because that outstanding nurse had eyes that actually saw that night she was able to help me. Our eyes are to see with. Try and soak in all the world is revealing and help where you can. Do not turn away.

I am quite sure I was post-partum all the way but not knowing or realizing it at all and certainly did not want anyone to know. Most Mothers would want to get out with their kids to the mall, grocery shopping or parks. That was hard with both my children but I knew I had to get out and not just sit in a place where the four walls closed in. I had to get out of my comfort zone. Our son's birth was easier because we knew of my propensity for protein in my urine. I chose a calm C section with an epidural. This was a much easier recovery than my first child. I was out of hospital in less than forty eight hours after our son's birth. He is an amazing young man today. I had my makeup and hair done on the second morning of my stay at hospital with our son and we were discharged shortly after. Children are such a miracle.

While getting out and about with two young children I still had to overcome fear with my feelings of inadequacy and a lack of confidence. One must force self to go to places that are not of great comfort in order to get better both mentally and physically. I mentioned that earlier and we need to become familiar with it. We have to go there a lot to get better. I missed the opportunity of talking with a professional early on and learning some coping skills to manage in my early motherhood. Do not be like me please ask someone for help. I missed the boat I eventually got on and my wish is that you do not miss a thing and heal sooner than later.

This is but a mere glimpse of what is removed from you upon being silenced in life.

Again it gets dished out and you just keep taking it. You know it is wrong but you cannot do a darn thing about it. I was recently on a trip with my daughter and we were shopping in a mall. We took repose for a bite to eat. The gentleman at the food counter I went to shorted me two dollars in change. I do not have courage to correct that so I just take my meal and sit down. My daughter is smart enough to know my body language and she asks "what is wrong Mom?" I explain what happened. She asked if I would like her to go and get my two dollars back. I said "no I have to do it" and I go back to the counter and let them know they gave me the wrong change and they just shrugged their shoulders. I walked away without my two dollars crushed in tears at fifty two.

With kids in competitive sports you get to go to a lot of sporting events. This one was gymnastics. We were in the tourist area playing tourist and purchasing souvenirs. Often I wish I could use the change in my purse. Many times I count out two or three dollars of change in my hand and then at time of purchase chicken out because it will hold up the sales person and their line. I am not of significance enough to do this. On this trip I watched what confidence is such as a young gymnast of fourteen take the thirty to forty five seconds at the cash and pay with change from her change wallet. She did not even worry like me and did not precount the change in her hand. This is real for me people. This would be a side effect of suffering from abuse or impact to one's life from dealing with trauma. I cannot return anything to a store for credit that would be a confrontation. Some of my family think this is funny. They cannot get there from here. They have not walked a mile in my shoes. People need to be cognisant of what abuse for a prolonged amount of time including formative years can do to a person. Always seek first to understand. We cannot judge anyone for it is not our place to do that.

A group of very close friends can attest to this. I partake in coffee reward programs. Great way to savor treats for free. My favorite the light roasted brewed coffee. After so many points you get a free reward. I wanted to see if the combo-lunch a great deal at nine dollars with what it includes qualifies for the reward? But I never have the nerve to ask. Wonder where that comes from. Could never ask in a class room and can never ask in life. I have been a coffee rewards member since 2012 and I would like to ask this question but I am too shy. About six months ago I finally asked because my friends encouraged me that I can do this. And no you cannot apply the reward to a combo item. It can be applied to the most expensive item within the combo. In case you wanted to or needed to know. Wow that did not sting too badly sounds silly I know. But when I master something like this I usually breakdown but now I do not. Rather I celebrate me. I can do this. This is large for me please understand I have a voice. I like what it says. It is a lifter upper voice not a tearer downer voice. I am taking control of my life because I will not be taken advantage of anymore. I matter. I can let people know nicely. I really can. We all can.

Lack of confidence would be leading the way due to love of self not being strong enough. With such simple events and happenings in my life we see that silence is occurring. Imagine when the events are magnified along with the stress levels and you can see the potential of how dim one goes. It is at this point when one climbs further inwards and become even more silent. It is so sad. I am very proud of myself where I was what I endured but mostly for where I am now. Safe and where I want to be. Now it is your turn.

Today the landscape is different. Today I was at the dentist for a cleaning. I sat down and read a bright neon board that said "like us on Facebook and show us the like at check in and get a free five dollar coffee card." I actually sat there for five minutes to get enough nerve to ask. But really I love my dentist and they love me. Of course when I showed them my like on Facebook I was given a five dollar coffee card. How nice is that? A year ago I would not have had the confidence to ask for the coffee card.

At the dentist when they spray your mouth with water during the cleaning I use to try not to disrupt or slow down the dental hygienist. I would limit the amount of times I would swallow. It was uncomfortable to have all that liquid pool at the back of my throat but I was not worthy enough to disrupt the cleaning. It would slow them down. There would be an awkward pause I cannot do that. I would not relax my jaw when they took a break for a second because I had to be ready. I did not want to waste their time. Do not worry about my discomfort it is only me the insignificant one. Today was different I made sure I swallowed so that I would not have that pool of water in my mouth. Many times I did that. The hygienist waited a fraction of a second each time. It is my comfort too. I relaxed my jaw each time they turned away to get something so of course my jaw was not tight. I am important and I do matter. Again this is large for me and I need to remind myself how significant each of these gigantic steps is for me. It is my credence in becoming stronger. Confident people have difficulty fathoming this or trying to wrap their heads around this. They have not lived for so long the way I did or the way someone has suffered from abuse and trauma their whole life has.

Old me validated and questioned all decisions. I am uber sensitive to all put downs slams tear downs and any form of bullying or harassment you see in life or in general. This I work on controlling or it will eat me up. Your reaction speed is hot, fast and hard. Your words penetrate like daggers. Oh man now you stooped to their level and you beg forgiveness and the pendulum swings the other way yet again. You are a very sensitive person. Some take this or crying as a sign of weakness and it is not. You question do you still love these people? You wonder what happened to them growing up that they think this is okay to do to other people. My heart stays here a lot. I wonder what is wrong with me. What happens if one never gets to the root of the problem what does that manifest too? The great Divine never gives up in life who the heck gives me the right to give up? I believed this grief was given to me as the biggest road block in my life and if I could solve it the rest would come. For me that means world peace.

In my world today the wounded need to get on the permanent highway to recovery. Many of the questions have been answered and many remain to be unearthed. I just did not realize how far I had come already. When compounded over life the impact is large. Which makes each step forward even more important to celebrate and to not be taken lightly but to be given the honour and party it and you both deserve.

I joined the United Church of Canada as a fifteen or sixteen year old. I did that under my own power and esteem with the guidance of a great Minister and the influence and guidance from my Mom. I am thankful every day for this. I can only imagine for those that do not have any positive influence in their formative years or forward years how much they suffer and endure. How scared alone and hurting those children young teens and adults must be. To yield them the power to start new is my wish.

I could not stand up for fear. Fear paralyzes you it makes life stand still. When inputs are not changed we cannot expect different end results though. I knew I was built for great things and not in a swelled head kind of way. I see now how lucky I was I got to see the light and I've come up from the abyss.

What is the impact of not telling my Mom a trusted adult back when it began at six and carried on until sixteen and then moved to physical and verbal attacks that culminated with an arrest? I was around thirty eight when I finally told my Mom. Why did I not feel strong enough to share? Could it be fear? I was threatened by the predators to not tell at a young age and why would I not believe them? I was scared I can remember saying over and over in my head as a child "I cannot tell anyone I cannot tell anyone." How do you out your family or someone close to it? Could it have been perhaps thinking my Mom or my family and friends would not believe me or would not love me anymore? Regardless the result for me I started shutting down scared to have an opinion or tell anyone.

I was a bit of a mischievous child. When my Mom would scold me and that meant raise her voice I would be so scared I would urinate out of fear due to what I had been through. But no one connected that occurrence. They just thought that was normal behaviour for a child getting in trouble for kid stuff I guess? I believe this to be a warning sign but no one can fault what one does not know or have capacity for or even be aware of such things in the late sixties early seventies.

Going merrily through life and something triggers a memory as simple as being at a church in one of the most beautiful areas in Quebec. A small rural white church that is well over one hundred years old with my Mom and Dad's name proudly displayed on the wall inside as part of the Sunday school roll circa 1930 something? Family from generations grace the cemetery. My parents married there in 1947 and shortly after that the church closed. The next marriage to take place in that church would be my sisters in 1972. That is a pretty neat statistic. A natural spring water stream is close by to fill your cup with the clearest crispest pristine water. The stream is close enough that when you are still you hear its beautiful angelic trickle in the background throughout the church grounds. Today it still plays host to three celebrations. Every year the community of yester year and new gather to celebrate in all its' splendor it has to offer. Each family adding to the magnificent bountiful community table of culinary traditional heritage delights. Gatherings are held each year in May for Mother's Day, July for Canada Day and October for Thanksgiving. There is no plumbing electricity or running water on the church property. Held together and made possible by many local volunteer heroes. My father was on the board. His brother was the caretaker and both my brothers help today to keep the history and connection alive. After the services and sharing of food was done my father would bring out his musical instruments. When I was old enough and had enough courage I would sing when my Dad asked so kindly to sing with him. He asked many times and for many years and I could not do it. Inside my heart I wanted too so badly but I could not have people looking at me or singling me out. I just could not. My Dad could see that I was visibly shaking and frozen in my steps during those years. I missed a lot of chances to sing with my Dad. I was blessed to finally grow out of this as a young teenager when I picked up the guitar and I learned to chord with my Dad and his fiddle. I had many a chance to sing and play with him after that including some talent shows we won playing together. It is not right for anyone to miss out on anything in life that is the bottom line.

    I take it for granted that everyone knows they need to try and move on. Keep going do not give up and do not be taken advantage of. At least I thought that is how everyone was built. But we are all made different so what works for one person may not work for the next person. I knew I had to keep trying. I knew I was not to give up. I did not know what I was facing or why but that spirit no one was going to extinguish it except me. It was meant to shine and so are you so there is no giving up ever. I am a cheerleader of life and people for today tomorrow and always.

When I get the chance to see a young person so confident I am happy for them and I am thrilled to have witnessed it. It could be as simple as watching a gymnastics competition with some of the people from my daughter's gym club. Or it could be watching a cheerleading competition also something my daughter did in her life. It could be a hockey game or baseball game for our son and watching the confidence of these young athletes. It could be other sporting events and you see a young person and they are crushing it. Being a person with some stage experience you can tell and feel that someone performing is living it and they own it. They are not being little hammy hams. Well maybe they are but in a good way. So much charisma and passion and they are not afraid to try. It is the same for that young athlete who you can see that the desire and drive is already within them. They are all in for everyone to see. They excel because they listen to instruction but most of all they are not afraid of failing. In my heart I know that young person believes in themselves and perhaps is also blessed to come from a family of encouragement and love. It warms my heart like no tomorrow. When possible I let that child know their confidence was showing and I tell them that they must have great role models in their lives. It serves no purpose to not share it back to the person that exhibited the great action. Let them know you saw their courage showing. I am careful to not say let your Mom and Dad know they raised you right because one cannot assume who are the role models in one's life. It is always best to be sensitive. My children hear that every day that they could do or be whatever they want to be. Equally when you see a young person perform a nice act of kindness there is no harm in letting them know you saw it and it was really nice to see.

I let a lot of opportunities slip through my hand because I was wounded. I was afraid to truly show who I was to show all of me internalizing was easier. Time is precious one must make the most of what is given or entrusted to us or it becomes such a waste. There is magic in all of us. Do not worry. It is in everybody and last time I checked you are everybody.

We all know someone who is okay to bring their pack of troubles to work or to life. They wear it on their sleeves and whine about it all day. Their whole life is negative. Almost like the world owes them something a chip on their shoulder you might say. I did not want to be like that. I never have been. When I see that I do think in my mind where does their madness come from? Why so much distain for life? Where has their darkness materialized from? Whatever the days occurrence was I love the song with the line from that songs that goes "no one knows what goes on behind closed doors" from *Behind Closed Doors*[10] written by Kenny O'Dell. Same for everyone though we do not know what they are going through unless we seek first to understand before we judge. It really is not our place to judge. Our role is to support and to understand. I made sure my stink from life would never come to work or out in my day. The people I hang with they do not need to hear that either they have their own things to worry about and to deal with. So naturally you just push it right off the radar. Let us just sweep that under the carpet like spilt milk and take it to the grave rather than to deal with how you are feeling. That would be the old generation thinking in my family. We need to collectively change that.

Regardless you go forward in your day and you try to get it out of your head. Some days it takes a bit of time to build yourself back up and some days you are not so good at building yourself up. Instead beating one-self up is justification for what you deserve! Wrong. If it is a good day you can push the horrible out so it does not eat your energy up and you are off to manage the world including the corporate one. This is not the right mentality. Close but no cigar. Close only counts in horseshoes. If I had of only dealt with the root problems earlier I would have lessened the impact in my life. I recognize that now and I have to accept that which I cannot control and look forward to the things that I can control.

Women in the corporate world do add another element of complexity. The number of women in prominent corporate roles is growing and this is good. Many industries however are still predominately male dominated. Mine is no different. In some instances you do see firsthand when a man complains it is being aggressive in the boardroom. When a woman does same she is deemed to be whining. Selling, working and sitting on boards with Municipalities, Associations, Not for Profits and Corporations you see a lot of back bench antics for lobbying for what certain groups want. For someone who is set for equality I see so much that is not right or quite on board. Again though I cannot be accountable for everyone's actions and I cannot let it get to me. Collectively we can make people, businesses and governments more accountable for what they do because collectively we all count. Everyone should be given respect. At this time however I did not push my point or opinion if it was not readily accepted at first. I did though let my work and work ethics speak for themselves and that has taken me far. Let's spin that one hundred and eighty degrees look how much I have accomplished. I was not firing on all cylinders as I was intended. I am alive now with purpose. We all have greatness in us waiting to be discovered.

Pick your poison of devastation some of the impacts look like too scared to tell too broken to belong too ashamed to fit in too dirty to see myself too controlled to function well. Perhaps you are living in fear paralyzed oppressed some or all of the above or other. Oh sick tummy it is time for you to be gone. Tick off this box for everything that applies to you. No joke seriously. Does this sound like you it sounds like me!

The impact on choice of friends is clearer now looking back. Not feeling worthy you go looking for the marginalized kids in school because that is where you think you deserve to hang out or you gravitate there. Impact and decisions really come into effect here. I have a great Business Degree a Bachelor of Commerce Honours. I graduated Cum Laude 3rd level honours with a B$^+$ seventy eight percent average. Not bad for someone who skipped so many classes in high school. I worked hard in College and University. I am a creative person stuck in a business mind. I am good at what I do. I try the best at anything I touch it is who I am. What about loss of income? The impact of these events made me sell myself short in life up until this turning point. I must let it go.

I love the arts singing, dancing, acting, and public speaking. I like to impart knowledge and help. I could run away on stage. Even in my professional job of marketing I get to coach and mentor in direct marketing and I have served this industry my whole working career. Performing speaking and imparting a story by any form of art be it by dance painting singing writing or other is so magical. Helping people gives a natural high.

The impact of growing up living and eating abuse on a daily basis leaves a path in your life similar to that of a hurricane. It is totally unexpected and always out of the blue. Never knowing quite when to expect it or know when it will hit but knowing it will. So you brace and prepare for the onslaught to come. It is a swatch of destruction high wide and deep coarsing through your veins and its ghastly beat brings torrent to your heart and soul. But today I know there is hope. The awareness, accepting and understanding has been building in me and helping me ease all hurt against me in my life and in finding my full voice. I now have a higher calling or purpose to help others in need. What is your true calling? With a full voice finding it is a lot easier.

TRAPPED INSIDE

STOP

Stuck in the spin cycle you realize for the first time or perhaps again that things are way out of control. But you are lost. You barely recognize it now. It just seems all so normal. Like an airplane on auto pilot. You are definitely acclimatized. Some of the people in your life have stopped hanging with you because of the stigma associated with you. There is a list of other things like low self-esteem, controlling people, and derogatory statements that are meant to keep you down. Meant to control you and of course impossible to break free. So you think about what to do but you never find a way to get out of the vicious cycle. At DebbieMajor.ca it may surprise you exactly what you have been up against as you try to gain the courage to break free. When you see the list of things holding you back in black and white it is very revealing. There are ways to overcome the barriers that are holding you back.

There were many days and years that were very dark where all I had were my thoughts. No matter what I realized really young that no one could ever take my thoughts away. They could remove everything else away in an effort to control but no matter how hard anyone tried they could not steal my thoughts.

Back in 2000 I wrote a song including a melody which is meant to show what kept me going and not giving in or succumbing in life.

My spirit could not be dampened. I owned what was inside of my head and for many years I worked on my plan for world peace in my head. Today it begins with my journey of encouragement, love and support for others to begin the real journey of their life. I do however picture someone like a Shania Twain type artist singing my song. Even better would be recording it with her or someone like her to help kick start a new charity to find and help all the lost voices.

LOST VOICE

Here is my song

"Baby You Can't Have my Thoughts"[11]

You can kick me
But you can't crush me
You can't keep me down
Life's too short
Gonna have some freedom
Baby you can't have my thoughts
Oh Oh Oh
Baby you can't have my thoughts

See me watch me
Grow night and day
Bella gonna make it count
Huh baby don't you cry
Baby time to fly
It's peace and solitude that's new
Oh Oh Oh
It's peace and solitude that's new

And you can kick me
But you can't crush me
You can't keep me down
Life's too short
Gonna have some freedom
Baby you can't have my thoughts
Oh Oh Oh
Baby you can't have my thoughts
Oh Oh Oh
Baby you can't STEAL my Thoughts (no way no how)

BROKEN AND WITHOUT A VOICE

When you get to this point you have no recollection or glimpse of identity or why we even exist. It is crazy madness and it is hard to make sense of anything as we go spiralling further into despair.

Most days you are walking on egg shells. Not quite sure what or who will get set off by what or by whom and what the outcome will be. It can be a walking time bomb so volatile and just waiting to explode. What would the word of the day be today? The merry go round that just keeps going and you cannot get off. It is like the saying from the movie *Forest Gump*[12] "Mama always said life was like a box of chocolates, you never know what you're gonna get." So you walk the line of Miss Congeniality or Miss Switzerland the glue and the calm that holds it together. You have compromised you for your whole life. Yes I have. Will you compromise you for the rest of your life too? You walk away to avoid any further incident. Are you weak indifferent or frightened? We need to figure that out.

I worked with a counsellor through a work employee assistance program. That is what got me to safety in my life. It came down to not respecting me enough to make sure I was safe. Every person on this earth deserves to be safe have food water shelter and love. There are boundaries and barriers that people cannot cross and they will be the ongoing protection now. A blanket to cover and protect like our basic rights as people and never to be taken off again! These two things along with awareness and open communication in all relationships for life are so important in order that nothing ever gets out of control again. To be used as some of the pillars of *your* new plan.

I still have many questions: how come some get out and others do not and how come some reclaim their spot in life and some never have a say are a few questions? In this past year being a student of Kary Oberbrunner and having the opportunity to take one of his many courses such as *Elixir Project Experience*[13] has made me strong enough to complete the first leg of my new journey. I now possess the right tools to answer many questions and make the connections and offer more help. I have learned so many things about taking action with purpose. There shall be no more wasted steps in my life. Some of the learnings I already knew I just did not live them or know how they connected. For example I am the power of positivity that is what my vibe is set to. It is the eternal light in me. In Kary's Oberbrunner's *Elixir Project Experience* he calls it the "RAS filter" the "Reticular Activating System". Different parts of our brain process information differently some is part of our conscious others are part of our subconscious. Some refer to it as our minds eye. We receive back in life what that filter is set to. We get what we put out in life. My internal one has always been set to positive. But if it is set to look for negativity or bad luck then that is all you get and see in life and in people and their actions. We all know that negative person and that is all that comes out of them their whole life. The person who says if it wasn't for bad luck I would have no luck at all. That person just needs to set their minds eye or "RAS filter" to go looking for the good.

It is not a nice feeling to feel trapped like an animal held captive. There is no option but to break free and get to safety it is not negotiable. You and your life count too. You are important. You need to break the cycle and getting help to make it happen is good.

WARPED REALITY

BARGAINING

In this hot mess living a life of panic and chaos is not an option. It is a waste. I am done bargaining in my head to make it okay in my world. It is a twisted reality when you try and make it okay in your head. Sell yourself first in your head and make it right then you can sell the world your soiled spoiled goods. Continue to be the victim by lying in "BED" and blaming others, making excuses and being in denial. This is also a model from Kary Oberbrunner's *Elixir Project Experience*[14]. Or be a victor and take ownership, accountability and responsibility for self and ones actions.

A victim lies in bed

B = BLAME
E = EXCUSES
D = DENY

Or you can choose to be the victor as in oar

O = OWNERSHIP
A = ACCOUNTABILITY
R = RESPONSIBILITY

I do not think anyone loves walking on tip toes. Wondering what is going to be the next phrase or word of the day that sets it off. So you just do not say anything in hopes of not sparking anything up. You hold back and keep everything to yourself. You talk yourself through the crazy hectic heated scene. Not too healthy. There are hundreds of scenes and you can make an excuse for all of them and you can make them fit how your head feels any day of the week. But is it healthy? I mean is it really healthy? I can fake my brain into believing anything. Or simply just run away. No that is not an option you have what it takes to manage.

The compounding effect of abuse has to catch up and manifest itself somewhere in your life. It will not hide forever unless of course you pick the option of shrivel up and die. But that is a real waste of you. It comes out in attitude and you may have heard these or seen similar attitudes before like oh poor me, the world owes me something, and people appear to have this big chip on their shoulder. Some explain it as a type of syndrome whatever you want to call it in life a vibe or an aura. With this big chip on my shoulder my personae out to the world and people was dismal dark and cynical and that was miserable with a capital M. Ugly world therefore ugly me. Some go through life never realizing how they look to others. Some would say that is short sighted but I just think people have never had the chance to get feedback on how other people see them.

Another barrier or hurdle to coming to terms for me is that I grew up with God in my life. And I can tell you God does not give up. God never turns his back on anyone in life. So who the heck am I to turn my back on anyone? My whole life is about kindness being kind or how I coin it *kindbkind*[15] which means kind onto kind or meet kindness with more kindness. There is good in everyone. Sometimes we just have to wait longer to see it that is all. I pray harder for the lost ones I always have.

    I told my Mom one day in my mind I know that I am a big part of bringing peace to our beloved Universe. Would it be me or threw me that peace joy and happiness wash the Universe? I know I play a big part in it. So if I am Universe and Universe is me then how do I walk away? Universe does not walk away. My Mom just listened. Truly we are all Universe. We come from the Universe. I understood recently that Universe does not wish us to fail but rather to succeed. It is true and simple and so it shall be done.

    I thought that if I could fix the broken in my life then the rest would come. That fixing the broken would fix me. Some will never realize they are broken that is the problem. You can bring a horse to water but you cannot make them drink. And for sure we are not responsible for anyone else's happiness another hard lesson to learn in life. I am responsible for my own gladness in life no one else is. Somehow deep down I knew this but you try to bring and keep the peace throughout no matter what. I rationalized until it sat right in my head and heart. I only just realized this for good not even a year ago. I am not accountable to others but only to the Lord, Universe and myself. Others are accountable for themselves no matter how hard others try and make you accountable for them.

    I get to spend time during the year with a very great group of girlfriends. Sometimes the best therapy is just good friends who will listen. Well this is an exceptional group of girls. All are very caring souls. The core of this group is four beautiful people who have been together for over thirty years starting in public school. These four ladies and this entire group are great role models for our families and for our communities for what caring and kindness should look like. One of the girls drove home about a family situation in her world and the way she expressed it to me resonated once and for all with me. I was not responsible for other people's happy end of story period. In this particular instance it was a family member struggling with substance abuse. No matter how hard you try to help someone the person has to notice first they need to change and then go about the process of changing. Our words may be enough for some to enact but may never be enough for everyone to take that first step. Our words should always be supportive words and words of encouragement but the ultimate accepting and hard work to change has to come from within. We can help you see all the good you have in you and the worth you have. Ultimately you need to believe too in order to see it through to fruition. I am not able to make people see themselves as they truly are. People have to be open and honest. They have to be willing to look at self and access the situation and make changes accordingly. I have learned so much from this group and I cannot wait to see what else they will show and help me with.

You can live a life of fear and what you see is what you get. It will not change. You can bargain all you want in your head to make it right. Bargaining is alive and happening and do you really want to do that to yourself for eternity? Or is it time for action and seeking help and doing what you have known is the right thing to do your whole life. Some great places to start can be found at DebbieMajor.ca

Stop suffering and get to a safe place. There are physical and mental boundaries that people cannot cross without consequences. All actions have consequences in this life or the next one or for other generations to come. Leave a great path for those to come behind you or with you to follow.

BROKEN AND WITHOUT A VOICE

The best virtue in life is you. You have all you need. There is better there is more and there is whole. I am almost there. It is a magnificent feeling. Why settle for only a shadow of your whole self? Deal with the struggles once and for all and set yourself free.

BREAK THE CYCLE

HOPE

In your heart you do know that you deserve a say in the world at your work with your family and friends and your significant other. To this end you know on some level it is not acceptable and you know you have to recognize and admit it has been blocking your freedom. Blocking your ability to have a bountiful journey in life with voice of full regalia!

    I have not figured out everything yet. I believe that is an ongoing progression in life to learn apply live and auto correct along the way. Make adjustments with checks and balances to right the course if need be. But for some issues I have been shown the path and wellness of self is top of mind. I am starting to be healthy and stronger and this is definitely an asset to moving forward. I have some remaining blockers in my life holding me back. I need to make my whole family aware of what happened and what really went on. I know I have to manage these before I will truly experience freedom and my full voice. I know that Universe and Lord have revealed to me the things I need to make this happen and I have full trust in my ability to handle this.

I do not question my love for my husband, family or extended family and friends it is pure. I have yet to truly understand where the anger of the people who inflicted this agony on me comes from. I do hope one day I can. It would assist with my healing and closure but is not within my control so I cannot fret for long over it. I do not wish harm to anyone. I only wish warmth love and healing so all may live a healthy and full life. One filled with action, purpose and direction. And so I soldier on with love and light only. It is much better not perfect but definitely heading the right way.

I want to be a great role model for Universe, for myself, my family and others but mostly for my children. I wish them to be aware the impact they have taken in over their lives and some of the side effects that they may have to manage going forward. I want them to live the fullest life possible with no burdens left over from childhood. I must therefore do the right things now not say one thing and do another. Actions must equate to words. Have you ever noticed in life most people's actions and words are not in alignment and it is okay to let people know nicely when you come across this?

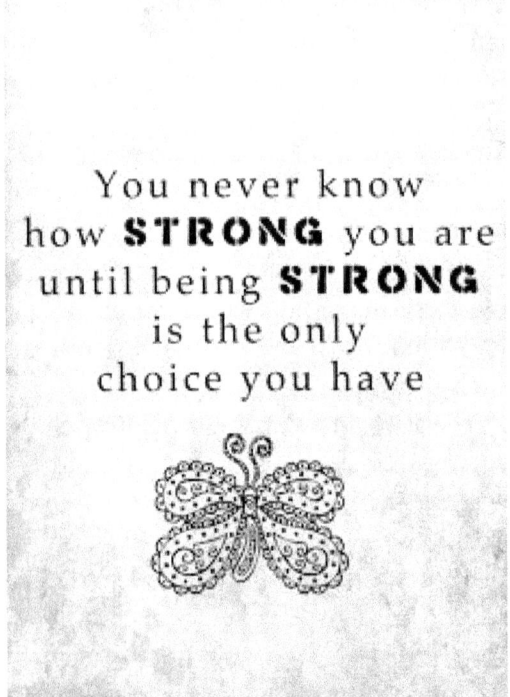

16

To be honest my husband and I built confident children and they stand up in their lives and have since very young. I hope we had some influence in that. They each had great role models and mentors in their lives with their sports coaches and teachers. They reinforced basic life skills like having great work ethics, dedication, perseverance, focus, drive, camaraderie and showing our children what it is like to be a part of a community and to give back to that community.

I am open and honest with our children and I let them know when they teach me something which is often. They do however have trouble understanding long term impact of abuse on people not having been through it and what it can do over extended periods of time. But they understand more and more each day and are accepting of where I am at. I adore them. My love for them is unconditional.

There is no hurt and sorrow in my life anymore. I cannot stress enough you have to get to a safe place. We are different people some are nurtures and some are me centered. There are always exceptions and varying degrees of each. I rejoice in the uniqueness of everyone it is to be embraced. Uniqueness is hard for many to embrace. If it does not fit what they call normal they deem it weird. But the opposite of weird is common and I do not wish to be common when we are all unique. That would be boring. No one has to rain on anyone else's parade either even if it is a parade of one. We support and cheer on the parade and give them encouragement. We celebrate them because they have found their special gift and are no longer listening to all the negative voices in their head. They are listening to one voice theirs and it is saying "oh yes I can."

I have some child incidents to share with my family and this represents the last blocker to my final release from a life full of torment, burden and shame. In final anticipation of what true freedom will look and feel like in all its glory and splendor. I am so deserving of this wholeness and I cannot wait for this part of my life to be closed and the final release of my life back to me. To open up without first making everyone aware is ethically wrong. But knowing it needs to be done and will be done is cause for celebration enough. I was not ready in my life to face this hurdle but I know now with the grace of God, love, dignity and respect I can now confront my deepest darkest evil secrets and not feel quite as dirty about myself as I use too. I now embrace and rejoice in each small step taken. This is a true celebration of me and I know you can have a true celebration of you too!

BUILDING TO FIND YOUR VOICE

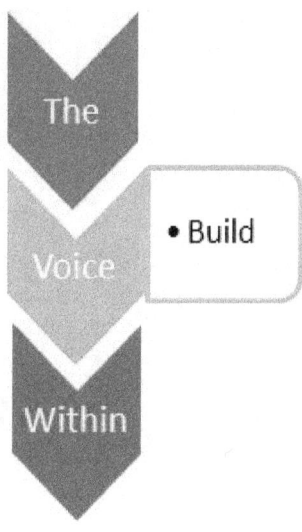

*If we keep spreading and giving love
it should make it around the world and back
for us to see and feel* [17]

COURAGE

TO GET TO A SAFE PLACE

It begins when you are in a safe place to grow and change. Safety is paramount. Living in a place of peril is not acceptable nor an option. Children are like sieves they soak everything in. They begin to think and believe what they see is how adults should act. Then they go looking for adults who look and have like characteristics as they have grown up with. The cycle never stops. Realizing that it is generational is great awareness. Generations before were messed up. The one I am in is messed up. What are the chances that the generations that come after me will not be messed up too? How about the generations not even born yet? That did it. The straw that broke the camel's back. Someone had to break that cycle or take the secrets to the grave. I choose to break the cycle and bring more awareness to the issues. Yes it took counselling. At that time I could only manage therapy for the sake of the children not for my own sake. Courage to involve authorities and manage through the process of healing can be overwhelming. The consequences of living a normal life are at stake if you do not deal with the issues at hand. In the long run it is the right thing to do but that in of it-self took fifteen years to enact upon. Yes it was hard work. It becomes about how bad do you want change in life? It is extremely rewarding when the pieces come together in life as it should be with much excitement and fanfare. Each day is a joy and blessing. You put your feet on the floor because you want to not because you have to.

Find a safe place even if it means you have to call the authorities go to a local shelter get help from a local organization visit a family member or visit a friend. Safety is first then to build the confidence self-esteem and self-worth. If you are at risk though and do not get to safety it is not possible to get to the next step. The statistics are alarming and increasing all the time. According to Canadian Women Foundation's *Infographic* "What's Happening to Our Girls"[18] forty six percent of girls in Ontario high schools are victims of sexual harassment. The statistics for all children are astounding and from Statistics Canada we learn "In 2009 the rate of family-related sexual offences was more than four times higher for girls than for boys. The rate of physical assault was similar for girls and boys." The fact is that assault and violence against any child is wrong.

Having to manage barriers or being prepared is hard to handle in the heat of the moment. But having a plan goes a long way. Along with the *Infographic* from the earlier chapter having things like a bag packed a list of phone numbers in case your cell phone is taken or stolen your own bank account and a list of support places to go or call in case of need are other items to consider in your plan to gain the fortitude to get to a safe place. There is a checklist for being prepared at DebbieMajor.ca

LOVE

FIRST TO UNDERSTAND THEN TO ACCEPT

With no voice only I can stop my suffering. With every great recovery or rebirth comes the epiphany of total acceptance and love for self. Acceptance for where you are at today in life. It will only work if you arrive at this one hundred percent with no wavering or doubt. Correct, change and augment but no more jumping off the band wagon! Total love of self is possible. Yes support and encouragement are benefits but the hard work and grit and all of that comes from within. It comes from nowhere else but inside you. It comes down to how bad you want it. How bad do you want freedom or a change or a chance at normal? How much do you love yourself or wish you loved yourself? Or resolve to forever stay stuck with no hope of moving on. At some point in order to move forward working through things with a professional will get you there faster, safer and equipped better in life to continue to propel forward.

Waiting for fifteen years until it felt okay in my head to go see someone is wrong. I had rationalized it well enough and I was okay with it so I thought? Why wait so long? Trusted friends are a great place to start but getting help when needed is even better.

Not sure why we are our own worst critics. I do not need any help in beating myself up. I do a great job all on my own. Beat yourself up looks like how can I be so stupid so naïve how could I not value me or have enough respect for myself to do anything? I did not value me. And now I realize I am priceless. I just realized I had to change the talk track in my head. The only place I am master of my own domain. In my world there is only one way to do things the right way. Why create a new wheel? Why not augment the wheel and take what you need that fits for you and toss away what does not fit. But why make a new wheel? Beating me up is hindering the wheel not augmenting the wheel.

A soul sister shared a story with me one day. She had opportunity to ask a question of her Grandmother who was probably in her late nineties at the time and her Mom perhaps in her late seventies or early eighties at that time. With my friends children that is four generations. How fantastic is that and it is just so remarkable in of itself. I shake my head in marvel each time I have an opportunity to witness that or hear of that. My friend had the chance one day to ask both ladies when the best time of their life was for both of them. I am not sure if she asked them together or apart but both ladies replied from the age of fifty to seventy were the best. Of course my friend asked why and the answer was that they had taken care of everyone or everything in life that they had too and that time was now theirs. My friend asked why was seventy the end of what was the best times? Both said typically health starts failing at seventy and you cannot do all the things that you use to or wanted to.

BUILDING TO FIND YOUR VOICE

The window of life is short it is precious with not one second to waste.

Like a light switch I flipped it on or off. Change on a dime is another way of putting it. I made a conscious effort in my head to not say negative things about me. I allowed myself to say oh I can do better I did not handle that very well but next time I will and I say thank you for giving me or allowing me to see the lesson that is before me. I had to catch my thoughts a thousand times and flip it. I had to tell myself to stop it. Why do you say that about yourself? Why do you take yourself down that path of destruction? I own my head space. I own my thoughts. I own where I will set my subconscious too. I am good. I can contribute. I am smart but most of all I am okay with me. I accept all the bruises and bumps I have had in my life. I accept the lessons that I have learned. I give praise that I have come through and learned so much about myself. I am proud of me. I am and will contribute more to life in a meaningful way that matters to me. I am important. I do count. And most of all I love me. I choose not to be sad that it took me fifty four years to get here. I am so thrilled and over the moon that I am here. I have thoughts and feelings wants and needs just like everyone on this earth and all thoughts and feelings matter.

I am not a therapist but I do know it is important for people to love them self. I do know that we are all useful. So it is okay to spend some quality time here and to have people help solidify and strengthen you. There are a lot of years of bad thinking to undo. We did not get here in one day nor should we get out in one day. But the beating up of oneself must also cease or moving forward will be near impossible. We are our own worst critics. We never cut ourselves a break or any slack. If we look at culture from twenty thousand years ago we still have a lot of wrong to undo. We have come a long way but there are countries still today where a person must walk behind another person. We are all equal. We do not have twenty thousand years to turn the thinking around on this or on violence, trauma and abuse. It is a short window to fixing the problem. So we have to throw that light switch on or off and not take twenty years to get there. We have to get moving now. There are things that we can do to not beat ourselves up so much and begin the process of loving oneself and they are available at DebbieMajor.ca

My goal is that collectively we are better able to read and see peoples despair in their faces. I wish that we have the courage to ask why there is despair and find how we can collectively help. It starts with awareness to all that most people are walking wounded each day and we are unaware oblivious and in general we do not care. It is them not us type of attitude. So we continue to be walking wounded. We collectively share the same space. We all breathe the same air. We are responsible for the same world why then would we not care about each other?

With love comes acceptance of who we are. What we have done in life and all our experiences. Also what we wish to do and to be proud of everything we stand for. Loving one's self in one's own skin and being okay for the world to see and hear is tangible and it is achievable for you.

It is a beautiful place to be. We do not remember to have a party very often but we should. Work family other stresses take most of our time each day. How about fifteen minutes a day to step outside to feel the sun on your face look up in the sky and say one hundred times I am beautiful inside and out. I share openly the message that each of us are beautiful inside and out. There is beauty in our family, neighbourhood and where ever we go. My therapist challenged me to do three things each day just for me. Not grandiose things simple things a hobby, sleep in, read a book, sip your coffee outside, go for a walk, exercise, work in your garden and be kind to you are just some of the things we could do each day for ourselves. We usually are kind to everyone else except ourselves why is that?

I now accept and praise who I am what I have done where I am going as a splendid offering to the world to be shared. I will work hard in life to be the best and as whole as I can be otherwise for me I would not feel fulfilled and I will not be at my best to help others.

Understanding me was hard what is important to me in life? We are all different. What makes me who I am? All great questions I think. My Mom is a very giving person. The opposite of selfish she is. She would help those in town who needed it most. In many ways I am like her. It gives much delight to help in any way. Sometimes it can be as simple as a smile to a stranger or helping an elderly person with groceries to their car. I do not want in return. I help people each day at work with great marketing ideas. I give freely of my knowledge so others can advance. I am not worried that they will get better than me. I am genuinely happy when someone works hard and succeeds in life. I am not angry or sad that it was not me. I rejoice in them.

I was forty six years old and I remember standing on the bottom steps of our stairs in the family home coming down to the main floor. A light went off and I defined my justification in life as three words *to help people.*

I ran with that for many years as I was fulfilling that through work and in community. I was helping corporations, government and organizations. Efforts and hard work usually pay off. I was helping in my family to try and keep the peace and play Miss Switzerland at the same time. I am made to help. But full love of me would not come for another eight years. I listened to all the nay sayers who could not see my love to help and heal inside of me. They thought it was naïve. I listened to other people get me off my true game because I did not love myself enough. Without love there is no conviction or passion. I did not respect that I matter most. I listened to the voices of no instead of the voice inside me that said yes until now that is.

We are all made for something and in loving and accepting oneself in all honesty and truthfulness the possibilities are endless. The world is our oyster. True jubilation and happiness are about to begin if we let it if we keep loving all of us. The answers and clues begin to unfold each step forward we take.

Stop and smell the roses, is a very important saying. That balance of life work and play makes us more fulfilled people and better able to manage what life will bring to the doorway of our soul on any given day. My husband brings this reminder to our marriage all the time. If he did not I probably would have missed our children growing up.

Upon loving oneself in all its glory and splendor the true color or spirit rises to the top for the world to see. At first you are in disbelief. Can it really be this simple yet so fulfilling? Absolutely I am living proof. Every day I learn more things about me that I adore and admire and some things I do not like as much. I will continue to learn to embrace more of me so I may show my love to others more as long as I am alive. My hope is you embrace and love yourself too.

ANGER
LET IT GO IT SERVES NO USE

Understanding the anger is ongoing and has to be maintained not attained is key to getting healthy and remaining healthy. It can present in many fashions. And it can be unleashed in many avenues as well. The best thing for health is to manage the turmoil. Ill temper can lead to stress, high blood pressure and many other body ailments. To understand where it comes from why so vexing and what the reasoning is behind the anger is needed to get you closer to that whole person of wellbeing.

I came to realize my ire was directed at myself. That I had let it consume me for most of my life with no positive outcome no change or nothing of substance coming from it. It was a pure waste. I was mad and angry with myself. I was angry that no one would stand and be accountable for their actions. I am angry at myself that I took so long to get healthy that I did not have enough respect for me. I am angry that people did not see my pain or ask why more often. Many people are in denial of their acts of darkness. Again it takes a lot of time to realize that their actions are not my accountability. I have finally accepted that. Through working with a therapist I am not angry any more but have to manage this anger on-going and must remember it is about maintaining it and not attaining it.

I will always continue my words of encouragement but the change and evolution is now in their hands where the control has been their whole life. It sounds harsh but everyone hears the same message and some take action with the message. I cannot make people take action. They have to do that for themselves.

I have love and compassion for those that have sabotaged and devastated me. I hope they have gotten the help to manage their anguish and confusion they have had in life. All distress and agony is wrong. It is up to education and awareness by all members of a family and community that will help in the long run to out and stop all trauma and abuse. Together we have to stop the pain and hurt for those most vulnerable the teens and young ones of the world.

I had such dreams and aspirations and goals set. Be successful with my world peace plan. Be successful with my family. Be successful at work become a millionaire by forty two. Buy my husband a sixty two Stingray for his forty fifth birthday were a few of them. You think people in your life in your inner circle would understand your ambition. Embrace it, help you or at least support your initiative. But they do not understand why you want to do what you want to do? They do not understand why you want to rock the boat? Why would you want to change things? Just fix your own back yard they say. Do not worry about other people. So instead of trying to understand you they tear you down with their harsh words and half-truths and you believe them. Once again you are knocked off your dream because you let someone else's input into your head. You halt, stop and retreat. You turn away from your dream with your tail between your legs. You try to explain you are not living up to your full potential. In your mind and heart you know you are made for more there has to be more in life this cannot be it for if it is I am one depressed angry person. They do not buy it see it and so support is usually not there in the true meaning of the word. Before I arrived here I asked everyone in my family if they needed my support in any way to achieve their goals. If someone had of wanted some help I would have helped them arrive at their goals first before I went after mine. They all said no. I told them that cleared the deck for me to work on mine. So many people thought and think I am off my rocker. Playing with one card short in the deck, no! Wrong I am just a person with a dream and a vision and not wanting to waste what I truly was put on earth for and will work through this anger and channel it and the energy to good use and with commitment. I cannot waste what was given to me and I know I can help fix the world so I start with helping people. If I did not do this it would make me more sick than I already have been in my life and this time for different reasons. I cannot be the only one who feels this way.

I got over being angry that I have wasted some of my life. I am scared that I do not have all the answers on how to move it towards what I am made for in its entirety but am confident I will figure it out one step at a time. As I take a step forward the next steps reveal themselves and it becomes much clearer the action we should take. I help people at work that is who I am so I think I am just supposed to accept that that is as good as it gets for me. I came close but no cigar and I should settle that this is what my life will be. This is my life this is my lot so I am always resolved if this is as good as it gets I will embrace and bask in the journey and path that is in front of me.

If I settle it is a waste of what the Universe is showing or revealing for me. This thinking worked for a while. But you cannot hide your true feelings. I had been held down without a voice most of my life. Ultimately I was not doing enough to make sure more people learned how to love self and realize true conviction in life. If I do not work towards this then I cannot get to the next step of helping the world more. Help people first help the world next.

Now I deal with the anger in many ways. Angry because I have been excluded from so much in life and now I have to settle. Why do I have to settle? Angry is not a good look. It drips out of you in disdain. It is ugly. It is not pretty. It is jaded it is convoluted and it is downright dirty. I can hear it in my voice still today at times so this is what I work on today in therapy. Every day we work on things to make us better more whole otherwise it is a pure waste. I am a continual work of art and we get better each day. As they say in love we are the hardest on the ones we love. I think this is true. We vent we unload and so perhaps we are hardest on the ones who will not try to fix themselves or even admit that they need to fix themselves. But I have to remember I have never walked in their shoes. I must remember they are hurt and lost as well. We never give up but shower them with our kind actions and love. We try to understand and we never judge.

I never could settle in life. It literally would eat me up until I die. For me I must move through it and achieve my full value before I leave this earth. Go big or go home I like to say.

I have to watch the triggers so I can manage better. For me a trigger is a put down. I am uber sensitive with the experiences I have gone through in life. I am learning to let people know that their comment has hurt me rather than to react and come back with a dirty zinger of my own.

Strong people do not retaliate only weak people do. That does not serve any usefulness. Two wrongs will never make a right. I try to understand where the person is coming from that said it as it helps to understand that person. Most times you realize it comes because the person saying it has no confidence in themselves. Most times they also have compromised or weak self-esteem and confidence and is often the only way they feel strong powerful or in control. My go to place is to pray for people like this in need. Pray that they can see that it is love of self that is missing and pray they get help and become strong and whole. So you shower them with more love what else can you do? More love more kindness more help more value so they realize they are worth their own weight in gold and they need to stop the pain love self and find worth.

Constructive criticism is one thing we can all manage as it only makes us stronger and better. No one is perfect and we are in a constant state of learning. None the less I have to watch how I react to being criticized. I do have to let people know that sometimes you can tell someone that they are doing something wrong by just simply saying have you considered trying this? Softer is always better no one needs to feel stupid or put down or less. We all have different strengths and weaknesses and often the people in front of us have what we are missing or what compliments what we have. Usually we are blind to see this.

We all know that one person who has that chip on their shoulder for whatever reason. They have been hard done by their whole life. They world owes them something. They are good people but they have struggled and the world owes them for their struggles it seems. They are angry all the time. They complain about how hard they have it how little they have and no one is on their side. To make it feel right in my space I lump people like this into what I call the especial group. Especial is a word I made up and it means you belong with the group of really special people. They are better than other people so they are "especial." The group that does not have to follow the rules because they are so much more than the rest of us and their time is way more important than ours. I am good if you put your hand up and say hey world I am special and here is why? No one ever does that. You know it could be a person who does not park in the parking spot at a mall. They have to park in front of the ATM bank machine and block one lane of traffic and make people go around and create a big back log of cars. That use to bug me but it is not my accountability and I feel sorry for them. I pray they solve their sorrow and I try hard to send them off with a kind thought a wave and to send them off with love and a quick prayer.

    For me if you do not want to follow a basic 101 or basic rule in life then put your hand up and acknowledge the same. Let us know why you do not think the rules apply to you and I am good with that. No judgement that is not my place but do own the actions. Whether you speak the actions or do the actions they are definitely visible to see and feel by everyone. I ask this question a lot why do people think it is better to reinvent the wheel rather than to augment the wheel. I can appreciate and respect if you answer that because it helps me to understand you better and allows for clarification as to why. We know the rules say in life we should follow these steps. You choose to go in a completely different direction and you wonder why you are not getting the results you want. You have difficulty in acknowledging that you are not following the basic rules of life. This is cause for stress for me but we cannot worry about everything in life as it will eat us up alive if we do.

BUILDING TO FIND YOUR VOICE

The third eye is a wonderful thing or it can be a bad thing. When you set it to go looking for all that the world owes you, you see only the distress or hard ache of your life. Sometimes we live in that hard place our whole life not realizing it was actually us who put us in that purgatory to begin with.

You cannot diminish the bad. It happened. What would you like me or your neighbour or your boss to do? Give you a silver platter or a get out of jail free card like in the game Monopoly. Why? Because bad things happened to you, you should automatically receive good things in your life? No it does not work that way. You had bad done to you. You got a crappy deal in life but we have to make of it what we can. We are accountable to no one but ourselves as to how we manage finding happiness within our life. Will it take you down and define you for good. I hope not. Or can you honour it respect your past learn from your past what not to repeat. Realize what is the right thing to do is and move on to a healthy life and a healthy you.

The world owes us nothing you make of it what you want. You see of it what you want you take of it what you want and you heal from it what you want. Take that which you need and leave that which you do not.

Anger serves no point other than to take you down into the abyss of hell. To leave you there until you are ready to release it and the others who have mutilated you. Concentrate on healing self and the rest will fall into place naturally as our confidence continues to grow and shine each and every day.

EMOTIONS

STAGES OF GRIEVING LOSS OF SELF

It seems in order to be free one has to experience conception and the birth of something new like the new birth of oneself. Spending a life in madness is not where it is at. No matter how you slice it or dice it there is some grieving to do and to get through. As we Canadians know we are as unique as each snow flake so then is the process and steps or stages that one goes through on the road to wellness. No two therefore shall be the same.

Maybe we have heard of them or some of them before. Five steps, seven steps, nine steps however many steps to become whole. It does not matter how many steps. Many are the same some are similar. They all drive to the same end which is what is most important. Being of sound body mind and soul in oneness with much honour and respect of self is a great place to be.

One set of steps resonates with me from Dr. William DeFoore, Ph D. of angermanagementresources.com.[19] He outlays the steps of grieving as:

- Shock
- Denial
- Anger
- Guilt
- Pain and sorrow
- Release and resolution
- Return to the willingness to love

Usually the stages are used to grieve a loss of a loved one or a traumatic event. Here I am the loved one. I have totally grieved the loss of myself for fifty four years and I honour all that I have been through as part of my journey. All the struggles, anguish, pain, fear, hostility, guilt, shame, spite, revenge, rage and back again a million times or more. Pick your bruised battered body, soul, spirit and chest up. Hold that chin and head up high. Hide whatever happened. You spend the next while telling yourself that you are good and then as the provider of the home you go out and try and make impact. You want to make it count in the big bad world. I did it with a lot of grit and tenacity and perseverance. I talked to God and Universe every day. I let him know that this is not where I want to be in the world. This is not how I imagined it playing out. I just did not know what or how exactly it should be. I knew that the Universe does not give up on anyone or anything so how can we as humans give up on anything or anyone? We cannot but we can direct our energies and cause to people who are of like mind and who would like to grow and learn and become confident and in love with self. Surround self with people who have similar cause and can relate. Find comfort in similarities to know that we are not alone. Deep in my heart I know what is right and I know there is only one way to do things in life the right way. Why can I not though? What is missing? Me! I am missing I never existed.

My Mom is not a person who mopes around. It is of no use to mope around. I agree with my Mom. Why sulk for what you cannot have or do not have and instead be thankful for what you do have. I did not want to mope for my whole life for what I could have been for what was taken from me. I do not want to mope at all. I just want to get on and see whole happy people in the world and in my life.

I am in charge of my life. I own it. Just like I own my thoughts, I own my own happiness. I can sit in doubt, fear and hate or I can share more love share more kindness find myself once and for all and be myself and all that I want to be.

It does not matter how you get through the cycle. It just matters that you do. It does not matter that you have to go round and round a few times until it fits or you have final resolution, understanding, forgiveness and love. It does not matter if you change, modify, fix and correct along the way as we learn more about ourselves and become true to our real identity and stand up and have a say in life.

I lived in that cycle for close to four decades. I honour that I did. It is not with malice for I would not be where I am today if I did not go through what I went through. I would not be armed with as many skills and tools to manage the triggers in my life if I did not and I would not be able to offer help or support if I did not go through these things in my life either.

I am working through residual anger and long term Post Trauma Stress Disorder (PTSD) effects of my life. Where a few months ago I may not have realized some of the side effect as PTSD I do recognize those side effects today. Some in my circle have trouble understanding that things change in our path of healing as we become more aware or deal more with the hurt and pain we accept truthfully where we are at. If that becomes about understanding that I have repressed thoughts and suffer PTSD then I will embrace the learnings to get through this too. The wounds and scars only make me stronger and give me more resolve to bring fullness and wholeness to my life and to as many others as I am able to. They are just gentle reminders of where I came from.

To build up confidence in individuals, corporations and businesses of all sizes that I deal with in my daily life is very important to me. Everyone and every business require a clear voice and a clear message in order to succeed. If I did not cherish these lessons of life and of the past four decades it would truly be a loss of greatest magnitude and epic proportion for me.

Tell me as we go through a horrible event we actually say to ourselves can you believe that just happened. I tell myself I have more respect for myself than that. This is prevalent in any aspect of my life. Especially respect for self in a relationship, family, work, friends and community. But why it took so long to change that landscape to not have to go through any more horrible events is hard to understand. Bottom line is we do not love ourselves enough and keep letting it happen over and over again.

There is shock and disbelief of the event whether it occurred as a child or an adult. The root problem is not enough love of self in my opinion. So many times we make excuses to make it fit. We look for a way to deny it even happened. Some push the occurrences so far into the subconscious and then have a real struggle and a hate on for life and never get out of that funk. It hurts me to no end to see that. Please do not let that be you.

The constant beating up of oneself with the realization of being too weak to stand up causes such quilt. This eats at you and it does not take a rocket scientist to see the damage it does on our health. I am a walking poster for heart and stroke disease and it is not a modelling gig I am proud that I qualify for.

Some people call me nuts. I talk to myself when I have to. When you cannot talk to others for fear someone will make fun of you. Or you practice if you had a chance what would you say and you speak it out loud. It makes it not so foreign when you have a chance to get your point across or made because in your mind you have been through it at least once already. Creating things first in our head makes you feel like you have done a practice run. You have seen it once before already so it is not so scary. I have to imagine the worst of everything and then imagine the best of everything and then I know I can personally manage anything in between. I have seen it already and I am better prepared. Of course you have to find what works for you.

I talked myself through upheaval, sorrow and depression. We all know someone in our life that just puts out angry and complains about everything all the time. Rather be right than be happy. So bitter on life that there is nothing not even one good thing they ever talk about. When we are young and we are beautiful or handsome in looks and we have this outlook we may get away with it. But as we age and sometimes our beauty slips away and all you have is this ugly jaded look. It is not very pretty. It is etched in all the deep lines in their faces and their bodies they are hardened. I do not want to be that. I will give off light not darkness. I will try and see if I am being dark. I will change the conversation to see it in a positive light. I was built on my cup is always full. I count my blessing each and every day. I am so thankful for all that I have and have been given. I pinch myself how did I get so lucky that I have chance to live within this hemisphere. I have food, shelter and love that so many do not have. One must put it in the right perspective and frame of mind to forgive and forget. To remember there are at least one million people every day that would trade places with us in a heartbeat.

Am I going to take the ugly and hate to the grave or am I going to let it go? Do I release it feel sorry for it understand it or hold onto it? I choose to understand and then release it. So I dug deep and I tried to settle where the anger came from. To try and manage accepting the people who have harmed you means you have to be very open to a lot of scars and wounds. These scars and wounds have not necessarily healed you only thought they healed. Your heart and full on emotion takes you to where you do not want to go. But in order to heal you have to go where you do not want to go and deep down inside I think you already know that.

It takes way to much energy and emotion to deal which your issues so you bail. You come back to the top and you go again from each person in one's life who has inflicted misery or had some influence towards the day to day misery in your world. In each case I could find hurt, scars and wounds even grief in their lives too. I could see that the environment that they were in during their formative years was not the easiest and that many of them experienced mistreatment and suffering as well. It does not make the acts right but it does help explain the why or explain their actions. It never excuses the actions. It made my forgiveness easier though and to allow my healing to continue.

It becomes about honouring one self and all the heartache and turning it into something good. Making sure we take positive steps forward with meaning and direction for self, family, friends, community, country and world if you can. If that is what you were made for. I know I am. I believe a lot of what shapes us in life comes from the environment we grow up in or what you are exposed to early on in life. If lucky enough you have some good role models in your life to emulate and follow, observe and pick up the good traits and actions from. If not it makes it a bit more difficult that is all. Ultimately it does boil down to belief in self and full love of self.

I have tried with some to find out why and where their anger comes from? My first attempts have not gone as well as I know they can. But through that I realized I am okay. For all the misguided and misdirected souls I send only healing love, positive energy, and the hope they become whole with ability to work through acceptance of their own actions and love for themselves.

I have released all the suffering from me many times over. I have set it free from my body, soul and mind. I have made my point and feelings known to the Universe and to most all whom I am blessed to know and touch in my life. I realize it is not my burden to carry anymore. The sad thing is it never was my burden to carry in the first place. I do feel sad and have much caring, empathy and love for people who are still carrying their burden running from their burden or who have succumbed to their burden. Please let there be fewer people with torment in their lives within our collective community.

With strong resolution and building of a plan for so long I am ready to face my full potential and my desire to bring such goodness to this beautiful earth and all the most fantastic people within it. All from whom we can learn, teach, show, tell and help. I have so much love in me to give it would be a shame to waste. It is what I was built for. Out into the world with kindness and love we all go and it is amazing first what you see when that is what you give and put out. In turn you realize it has been there all along. The help and guidance you need has been there waiting for you to come and receive. The learning to love you so richly deserve is awaiting your arrival. You can find out more at DebbieMajor.ca

Whatever part of the grieving cycle you are in I can only encourage you to seek professional help to manage and acknowledge. Part of it will be to create your *personal progression plan* so you may move on to the really good stuff in life that involves a whole you and not just a piece or a glimpse of you. I am truly sorry for your pain and suffering.

Give yourself permission to start over with no regrets to begin a new life with who you were intended to be!

WORTH

THE GIFTS WITHIN

If we have told ourselves we are useless for most of our lives it is pretty hard to just turn it off and start saying we have value. Yes it is very hard but it is not impossible. At some point you have to decide you are worth it or you are not. I personally think we are the most precious thing on earth. So once you decide to move forward imagine you have an on off switch that you have to turn on or off. Every time a negative thought or a slam against you is mounting in your head you have the control switch in your hand actually in your head. You possess the power to turn off the negative thoughts immediately. No slamming you anymore only rejoicing in you should be allowed. There will be set backs but only because we have not learned the lesson in its entirety and we need to see the lesson or learning again. We never beat ourselves up. We accept that we needed to see the teaching again. Each step forward and back is growth in respecting ourselves. I have repeated in my head on my way to work for one hour straight many times over I love myself, I am worth it, I am beautiful inside and out, I have purpose, no one can stop me, watch me, I am good,

I can. I can I can I will I will I can I can I will I will. Many times those words were enough. Positive words are definitely a good place to start. I want healthy and whole really bad so off with the negative thoughts about self and on to positive thoughts. No worries if you get stuck just talk to someone. No pity party, pick myself up, dust myself off and carry on for the good not some time all the time. There is no option to throw in the towel that would be a pure waste.

If words were enough why are there still so many walking wounded? Because mastering the art of self-love is ongoing in life and is really hard if you never did it at all during life. And sometimes words are not enough and a professional is needed in order to help you sort things out. For me most times the words are enough. For some more love is needed from a professional. I have sought help several times throughout my life. They only enhance your healing process. You deserve to make the talent, knack and flair you were given work for you instead of against you. There is a free training to help find who exactly you are at DebbieMajor.ca

I totally own the space in my head. I am in total control where my thoughts go and how long to hang out there. Coupled with knowing in your heart the right things or the steps that need to be taken in order to get to the whole you is very important. I can beat myself up for not getting on the path of wholeness sooner but there is no reason to I am there now. I remind myself daily being here is what matters most. I do not let myself hang out in negative land for very long quite frankly it is a downer. It is a dark and dreary place. So why subject? Why would I continuously drag my heart, soul and being there. I know longer let people thoughts or events rent space in my head for free. I give them the get packing sign and give them the heave ho.

There are empowering self-skills in us ready to hone and maintain in life and not just to be attained and forgotten but maintained and lived.

We must remind ourselves daily of how great we are in all aspects. We are talking a big celebration here. Scream from the highest hill in town and speak of your accomplishments. We have earned the right. We do not have to be arrogant about it but we can celebrate and rejoice in us. We usually forget this part and just carry on with the heavy lifting. To work at blinding speed with no recovery would lead to burn out and exhaustion. The recovery part is as equally important as the emotional scar we have just come through. If regeneration is not allowed to happen the body and all within become weak tired and lends itself to sickness more. To go through an emotional event in your mind and to work it out on paper is very tiring. It is like you are living it again and again for the first time. It is draining and exhausting. Your body needs time to recover and replenish. I forget this and then I am not allowing myself to regroup replenish reenergize and rejoice.

Learning to love self is an ongoing journey as is honouring oneself. The whole journey of life though is about readjusting and realigning. Accepting that we do not have all the answers and based on what we know today we make some decisions and as we learn more we make better and different decisions. All are important in the trip of loving and accepting self.

Our own voice is the loudest in our own head. That is the safe place to get and earn respect. But why is this voice the loudest only in our heads. It really comes from lack of confidence. It is easy to see or to think I am confident. Look what I have been through. Yes I have made it through a lot of things in life and I know it is because of my hard work and my want to do things well in life so I have to celebrate that more for sure. Yes I can stay stuck and be sore that I could have been more and better but I choose not to. I choose to love all of me and get better and I hope you do too. The world needs all of us as strong as we can be. Just like an airplane you would put your air mask on first then help others. It is the same mentally we must fix ourselves first otherwise we are not as useful in life as we are intended to be. That goes for all of us. When I looked last time we all qualify. Nobody gets left out here. This is not an exclusive club it is the biggest club of all the world club of humanity. We all belong and it is a privilege and honour to grab your spot. It is available and waiting for you. It is the largest sandbox of all and the rules are still the same as when we were young. With my children growing up I used the phrase *play fair share be nice*[20]. I raised my children on those five words. I have had many adults say if all adult actions could fit one of those three buckets *play fair share be nice* wouldn't the world be a wonderful place? I would have to agree on that note.

Give permission to yourself to give birth to your newly recognized value and worth. So I have to quit whining and stop the negativity and beating myself up. I have to define in my life what is really important me. What is it that I may like to stand for? What does my legacy look like? Call it whatever you want your vision what you stand for in life what are the values that are important for you? Am I able to build and qualify any of my values so I can measure my progress yes I can.

What is your deepest desire what gets you up each day? If you had a chance to do anything in life what would you do? You start to realize that everything we need is in us already we just did not know it or realize it. The new story begins now. It is truly up until now. It has not been written yet. I am the author of my life and I am in control of it.

So are you. As renowned Author Coach and Speaker Kary Oberbrunner has shared many times in his *Elixir Project Experience*[21] most times it is not about "dream discovery" but more about "dream recovery" and getting back to the dream we had earlier in life before an event or person killed that dream. I would add killed the dream like a fly on your kitchen table. Splat!

> "Again, you can't **connect the dots** looking forward; you can only **connect** them looking backward. So you have to trust that the **dots** will somehow **connect** in your future. You have to trust in something — your gut, destiny, life, karma, whatever. Jun 14, 2005 *Steve Jobs*[22]

As you begin to connect the dots going forward one small step at a time it definitely becomes clearer. You see what your next step should be and what action you should be taking to keep your vision mission or deepest desire on track.

There should be no wasted steps anymore in your life once you have clear understanding of who what why how and where you are going in life.

The image we project outward is an image or composite of how we are feeling. You can project outwards a three out of ten or project a ten out of ten which exhibits a person exuding with abundant confidence. It affects our self-image and the one we project out for others to see. We all see and know that person who has such a great image and outward glow. I imagine they are at peace with themselves. A place I strive to be one hundred percent of the time. I am almost there so close I can taste it smell it feel it and hear it calling my name and encouraging me to love myself more. We all are in this beautiful world and blessed to be a part of. Now to rejoice in all that we are.

PREPARE

OF SOUND BODY MIND AND SOUL

It is startling to see the statistics about different types of suffering and the effects it has on people. Looking at the overall statistics of abuse in our society first in North America and then globally and we see it is horrendous and shocking. The statistics are stark and cold. The opposite of the beautiful people they represent I bet? Is this dirt going to tarnish the ability to shine? For some it is and therein lays the regret sadness and true depression for me? I am done being this kind of statistic. I promised myself that there would be no more events added to this landfill size of garbage. I do not wish these statistics to grow for anyone. We must help these statistics by understanding and learning the signs of abuse. Like *Neil Young's* song "Ohio, How can you run when you know[23]?" That would be shame on me then. It would eat me up to turn a blind eye. I do not need a spot light to perform an act of kindness. I would do the same action when no one is looking. Truth told there is always someone watching over us.

I beg from my heart please seek the help and resources you need to become whole. You do not have to be in distress like this anymore. There is a way out of the dark abyss. You may not know it yet but you have everything in you already. Use the resource centers in your community and find the people you feel comfortable to speak freely and openly about your wounds with. Until then you cannot begin the true process of healing.

From the Canadian Women *Infographic* "The Need"[24] on one of the following pages which can be found at Canadianwomen.org we see the statistics are alarming. Sixty seven percent of Canadians have known a woman who has experienced sexual assault. Sixty six percent of female victims of sexual assault are under the age of twenty and eleven percent is under the age of eleven. Are we to just turn an eye and let the torture and assault continue? Every six days a woman is killed by her intimate partner in Canada. To my mind that is just pure craziness and madness and we all know it must stop.

The abuse against boys and men is equally as staggering. At the Canadian Association for Equality which can be found at EqualityCanada.ca[25] they report half of domestic violence victims are men but no Domestic Violence Shelters are dedicated to men. It is time to debunk all the myths about violence. Men and boys are just as equal in relationships to being abused and any form of violence on anyone is just wrong in our society in this day and age.

The Need

67% of Canadians have known a woman who has experienced physical or sexual abuse

66% of female victims of sexual assault are under age 24 (**11%** are under age 11)

Less than 10% of all sexual assaults are reported to police

60% of women with a disability experience some form of violence

Every 6 days in Canada a woman is killed by her intimate partner

You are not alone. I have walked in your shoes. I have suffered as you have and as many others have as well. There is strength and support for you. I am auto-correcting along the way to an even stronger healthier me. Something that will be ongoing in my life and I know you can too.

Moving forward having a plan becomes a necessity. It is like a roadmap. A blueprint draft of what you look like and who exactly you are. A plan that includes your values, beliefs morals and ethics like a *personal progression plan*!

Maybe the plan has been cultivating for a while. Maybe it is a brand new plan. It does not matter. It all starts with being the strongest and mentally prepared as you can be.

Just like any great business you cannot be afraid to look in the mirror and see what you see. You cannot be afraid to hear and understand what other people say about your business. In the business world it is called a SWOT[26] analysis, and it stands for strengths, weaknesses, opportunities and threats. You have to be strong enough to handle and manage the answers. The answers will help strengthen the businesses position, value proposition and would be tied to overall strategy.

A lot can be said about the SWOT analysis. It can be transposed to the individual level. It can expose a lot of areas that need some tender loving care. What does that individual SWOT analysis look like for you? Take a moment and list your own strengths, weaknesses, opportunities and threats and this will help to form the beginning of who you are? Getting back to what is important and always top of mind is accepting where we are. Understanding we have the power within us to change what we have control to change and to let go of the things we do not have control to change.

From the age of twelve until a couple of years ago I would struggle with sleep. Three hours of sleep in a row was a good night sleep. To say I would wake up one hundred times a night would not be misleading. Also it was hard to explain but I would take a breath and I could never get a full one. So about every twenty or thirty breaths I would get a good one and I would say out loud wow a good breath. I did speak to my doctor about this when I was thirteen along with my Mom. The doctor encouraged me to just breathe that it was most likely anxiety. Maybe if I had of opened up about the truth of why I was having trouble breathing with either my Mom or the Doctor it would have been a different outcome but I cannot change the past. I would have this problem with breathing well into my adult life. It does become a vicious cycle and so detrimental to ones health to not have proper sleep. I know that now and will strive hard to never be without it going forward. It is a fundamental of wellbeing.

My plan began with sound body mind and soul. I know all the right things to do. My body was carrying extra weight. I know this made me inflexible inactive experiencing joint pain and with pain every day. I suffered with sciatica for over seven years and tendinitis in my shoulder and arm. My knees were swollen and sore. My daughter's boyfriend remembers for many years when I had to come down the stairs from the 2nd level of our house to the main level one stair at a time. My knees were to sore and swollen to bend. My shoulder pain was extremely bad one time and my family doctor referred me to a shoulder specialist to manage the soreness in my shoulder. Best thing that happened for me. This doctor explained he saw twenty five new people a day. Twenty were women and five were men. The men he could usually fix in three weeks. Sometimes the women needed a couple of rounds or six weeks. He broke it down into four things sleep, pain, age and anxiety. He could do nothing about age and he was not the Doctor to help with anxiety. He encouraged if I needed help with that to seek it. But he could help sleep and pain. Another missed opening to talk about the hurt but I literally was too embarrassed of myself as a failed person and mother to bring up anything or ask for help.

For muscle tightness he showed me that we have five major muscle groups. I am not science oriented but basically over our shoulder and down our arm down our back over our hip down the leg and over our knee. He showed me how to tell the areas that were tight. All five of mine were rock hard inflamed and hot to the touch. I had a softball size knot or lump behind each knee that is how tight those muscles were. When you squeezed the muscle around my elbow I would jump with soreness as it shot up my arm and shoulder. It is a vicious cycle too. Not getting the right amount of sleep each night means not enough of the neurochemical serotonin is produced in our brain each night to manage our pain the next day. Serotine manages our discomfort naturally each day but when there is not enough of it the soreness does not go away.

I was prescribed an anti-depressant to fake my brain into making serotonin as my brain had not made enough naturally since I was twelve. I took ¼ of a sleeping pill so I could get six hours of glorious sleep in a row and I took a major anti-inflammatory to reduce pain and inflammation. The Doctor warned me the drugs are very addictive and when I could squeeze my elbow with no pain stop the anti-inflammatories. The swelling went down and within ten days I stopped the addictive anti-inflammatories and within six weeks I had stopped the other medication and weaned off. Upon a few more visits with him and one six months later I have been sleeping six to eight hours in a row for two years now. I only have joint pain when I have overdone my exercising or have not had a great night sleep.

Regular exercise helps too but sleep is king and I truly appreciate the value of it for the first time in my life. You need to sleep. One cannot function rationally without it for any sustained period of time. Let alone a whole life time full. Just this one fix makes things much clearer and more focused. Now with one step of the plan under my belt the other steps are presenting themselves and it is now beginning to fit together better. You cannot make the best decisions for you if your brain is not well rested. My thinking and reasoning ability and my level of happiness and joy have significantly increased and are actually unbelievable. Sleeping well is like a runners natural high.

Naturally our brain produces five neurochemicals on its own. Norepinephrine increases our heart rate. Dopamine helps us with focus. Endorphins help to withstand pain. Anandamide elevates our mood and serotonin allows us to stick with something in spite of pain. Learning how to activate each naturally is another great way to a healthy sound mind and sound decisions.

Back in 2012 I asked my family for fitness things for Christmas. Great things like a yoga mat and ball and some weights. I started meeting my girlfriend in town and we would walk different landscapes each time. Some up and down stairs in the downtown core sometimes along the board walk in the town we lived in. We found every neighbourhood with a big hill and we worked up to a seven kilometer walk two or three times a week.

There is nothing like being outside and feeling the wind the air or the sun in your face and on your skin. It humbles you to be with nature and you realize you are one if you are quiet enough to hear its splendor.

We did really well with our exercise program and in 2015 we kicked it up a notch with a personal trainer. Over the next eighteen months we both learned a lot about the value of great nutrition and the effort and commitment needed to really succeed with your fitness goals. As you can imagine we are all different so here too there can be no one size fits all fitness program. Everyone has different goals and strives for different things. Rule one be kind to oneself and rule two fitness comes with no judgement. Next to sleep exercise is another anchor of the plan. After thirty one years of marriage and two children I have dropped over sixty lbs and weigh what I did when I was in my twenties. I will never go backwards in my weight again as this great feeling I have from being so active and healthy feels magnificent. I am better able to manage what life deals my way now and I cannot wait until you feel this good too and share that with me.

    It is okay to have a cheat day. But in the end you have to realize to get better at anything you have to go through some suffering. You have to remember back to those days of school where you would have gym class and good old fashion exercising and you would sweat your you know what off. Unless you are sweating off more than you are taking in with regards to fat you are not going to succeed. In the whole scheme I think good nutrition is eighty percent of the fitness plan. Here in North America a lot of us do not eat that well. I call white sugar and white bread white death. Learning what is reasonable for carbs, protein, fat, sugar and sodium for you is really important. Understanding that protein is energy and what is good protein. I love a protein smoothie after a workout and I have yet to master the green smoothie but I will. With my girlfriend we kept a schedule of twice a week with the personal trainer and then two or three more times on our own each week. Now for maintaining I like at least three or four trips to the gym a week or trade a gym session for a run around the neighbourhood now that my knees can

BUILDING TO FIND YOUR VOICE

withstand a forty five minute run. It is always a great day after you exercise.

My Mom gave us so much of herself growing up even if it meant sacrificing her sleep. Collectively we did not realize what affect that has on one's health. The generations that came before us were strong in a different way and that amazes me. My Mom is strong. But today we know as part of well-being the brain needs sleep to make enough serotonin to clear all the toxins out of our brain and to manage the pain of our joints the next day. Serotonin is just one of the five natural neurochemicals talked about earlier that our brain produces on their own. My Mom never had the chance to make serotonin and they say if you do not cleanse your brain of those toxins each day you are more prone to dementia. My Mom has had short term memory loss for about ten years. She is eighty eight and rocking it. A happy girl she loves and lives for our Lord and is thankful for every day and for every moment she is given. I am her she is our Lord and I am blessed to have her as my number one role model in my life next to the Divine. She is still sharing lessons today in her words but also by her daily actions for the world to witness.

I went to visit her one day at her lovely retirement home and one of her nice actions was showing. I was waiting for the elevator to come so I could go to my Mom's room on the sixth floor. A nurse rode up with me. She had a key in hand and pushed the fifth floor. She mentioned a resident had locked themselves out. I asked her if she wanted me to hold the elevator for a moment while she ran a couple doors down to unlock the resident's door. She said that would be so nice and thank you. She scooted out opened the residents door and popped back in the elevator to ride up another floor with me. She asked who I was visiting and I let her know my Moms name. She said "I should have known because your Mom does nice things like you just did for me all the time she is so kind." That is my Mom to a tee. She gives her help and love freely to all and does not wish for anything in return. She has done this her whole life. The act does not have to be extravagant it just needs to come from a place of wanting to with expecting nothing in return. My Mom enjoys life and giving and her role of serving kindness and you can see she has been at peace for all of her life. You see in how she holds herself holds another person's hands enjoys to sit and talk share and to listen and she remembers to be thankful. She is of sound body mind and soul even with her short term memory loss. I am thankful and blessed she knows us all by name and her long term pathways in her brain are still open.

    I adore all of my family, extended family and friends. They are all such good people. In my family Mom's favorite saying growing up was "do unto others as you would have them do unto you" from the bible. You could count on her down on one knee with her arm around your shoulder to share with you that our actions or words were hurtful. How would we feel if that was done or said to us and then she would say "do unto others as you would have them do unto you." Thank you Mom those are great words to live by and to remember today.

    This past Christmas my daughter's heart was so kind to think of this. We live five hours away from my Mom. My Mom has dementia so my daughter could not enlist my Mom's help right away. She asked my sister if she could have my Mom write that saying from the bible out a few times on a piece of paper along with the words I love you. My sister said in the moment my Mom was happy to be doing this for me. Well Christmas morning you cannot imagine the tears of pure joy when I opened the present from my daughter and son and there was a beautiful silver bracelet with that saying in my Moms handwriting engraved on the front. On the back in my Moms handwriting are the words I love you. I could spot my Moms handwriting anywhere. To have that message from my Mom was so impactful and to have it given in such a loving and meaningful way is a moment that will stay with me forever. Each time I wear it or touch it is so overwhelming. Such a thoughtful gesture a big thank you goes out to my children. The real miracles of life are the young for they represent the future. Let's make them as strong and whole as we can collectively through our communities, families and lives.

In addition I am finding out more about the choices in food we can make as part of our overall health plan. The choice if possible to buy organic and stay away from hormones and steroids or as I call it the dreaded genetically modified organism or the short form GMO. Many countries have banned genetically modified products. Canada and the United States have not yet and I hope they do soon. This to me is very much part of wellbeing. Here is my interpretation of GMO as a lay person the GMO seed I think contains round up. Here in Canada we banned the pesticide round up and we can no longer spray it on any plants vegetables or gardens and this has been in effect for quite some time now. Both for residential and commercial use we cannot find round up in any of our retail stores. It is very controversial what is actually in the seeds that farmers in North America plant today. We as North America should want to know the truth about GMO. As well sugar, salt and flour truly are white death for the body and mind. When the body mind and soul are fit there is more clarity around the decisions and choices you make about your life going forward. We do care about ourselves enough and are one hundred percent vested in ourselves therefore I feel we should not consume GMO.

I needed to start controlling more aspects of my life and this is one that is good at all levels and it is hydration. I still struggle with it today. Never drink enough water. Six cups a day and I rejoice I need to get that to eight cups of water a day and then more. Often the lack of hydration causes a headache for me or cramps in my legs at night. You think I would know better. I use to beat myself up over this but I do not anymore. I just know I am going to try harder because I see the benefit of staying hydrated outweighs the consequences of not drinking enough water. Elementary I say my dear Watson. It is a basic 101 of life and if I am not going to follow it there had better be a really good reason. I will not tear myself down over it. I am past that now. I will just do the right thing and drink more water.

Families, schools, and communities need to be armed with better warning signs and what to look for as children are growing up in regards to abuse and trauma. To ensure that our communities have the funding, resources and tools it needs to help more and to bring more awareness to trauma and abuse and the victims of it. When I reflect on how much verbal diarrhea I ate and endured I shudder and wonder why I did for so long. I did not have any merit or benefit or so I thought and that does not make for healthy living or wellbeing. I finally get that now.

With my weight well under control I have other fitness goals now. I would like to rid myself of those stubborn fat spots. So I work smart at targeting those stubborn areas. It feels good to exhibit control over some aspect of my life. First the sleep, weight, nutrition and hydration I am definitely pointed in the right way to full healing. Just these first four elements of wellbeing all of which are in my control have increased my quality of life and outlook on life. I cannot quantify it. I am never going back the other way not a chance. Old me is gone I took only what served my purpose and I left the other stuff at the curb in the trash container for pick up once and for all.

Where does the vision for the future come from? It comes from deep within. A dream or a vision statement is a great place to start. It can be simply writing a mission statement out for yourself and perhaps one for your family. It is even healthy to have children write their own vision or mission statement. What is it that we truly stand for? What is it that you want to achieve with the time you have left? At the end of the day and you are eulogized what is it you would like the people to say about you and the kind of life you led and the role you played in people's lives. In Kary Oberbrunner's Book *The Deeper Path*[27] you are encouraged to write your "Opus." An "Opus" is essentially your overarching vision your mission your reason for being. You can view my vision my dream at DebbieMajor.ca

With weight, pain, and sleep under control I cannot tell you how easier it is to manage what life is showing me. This in its self is a testament that I am on the right path to full recovery and I will always have this as a good solid base in my life. Together with my love of life, Universe, Divine, people and all its wonder I am so stoked to see how this all plays out. I am not worried and I know it is going to be much fun and with much love.

SUPPORT

THAT SPECIAL PERSON PLACE OR THING

As stoic as I am and as strong as I will my mind and body to be and as stubborn in seeking perfection as I can be I realize that I need guidance resources and ongoing support in my life.

Everyone deserves a safety net of love around them. At any point to rebuild and meet new people of trust in your life is hard. There is no point in not leaning on the people and the places with the resources, knowledge and experiences that are waiting to help us grow, explore, solve and become solid. So we can ultimately have more peace, triumph and exultation in life. Try and work hard on creating your group of support.

I have family and we are a bit scattered across Canada. We do great we get to see each other a least once a year and for some who are far it may be every other year. But to say you can share a meal with all your brothers and sisters each year is remarkable. We restarted our family reunion that my father and his brother ran for years on the farmstead. We pick one day in August every year and as many that can come do. We play fun games and have a great family picnic. Our 2017 reunion is planned for August and it is going to be so nice to see everyone. It is a chance to share a meal and be all together which is very special indeed. We support and love one another and these are spectacular family memories to be cherished. I can speak a bit more freely with my younger generation siblings but I do have a unique and special bond with each of my brothers and sisters and their families. We all support love and have much admiration for each other.

Friends are the treasure chest of gold in life. There is no judgement among friends only support and one is welcome with open arms. We are all of like-minded people in the circle of friends. A place where one is safe and all views are encouraged and accepted even if not your cup of tea. No one rains on anyone else's parade. And it is okay if it is a parade of one. A place where you can be picked up literally or in spirit any day of the week and time of the day! A place where love is given freely and love is received freely and there are no strings attached. This is a beautiful group of girls who hang as much as we can and go on as many adventures as we can. I am so blessed and thankful to be a part of this special group because our connection is more aligned with each other each growing day. I have known these ladies for over fifteen years but was welcomed to this group eight years ago. Such warmth from these girls and they have helped me over a few of my hurdles I hope I have assisted them too. One of these girls while sharing about an upheaval in their family either about a brother or a sister in distress in their life and the way it was explained made sense to me. It finally hit home unequivocally we cannot be responsible for anyone else's happiness. I had heard it before but that day it hit home so hard. This is something I have to keep at the forefront of my life and worth repeating.

Work is sometimes a mini support group onto itself. A talented group of people who get the job done but have such wonderful hearts and are so caring and compassionate and great people I have the pleasure to work with over the years. You stand in the trenches with them day in and out and you have to work together for the cause of the client through thick and thin. You get to learn a bit about the people you are with. I have known some of the people I have worked with for close to twenty five years. One has held my daughter when she was eight months old. My daughter is twenty four years old today. The employees are great people where I work. They truly make the place.

For some support comes by taking your mind off of something. To immerse yourself in a hobby that takes you away. For some it is their art class that is a sanctuary or picking up a guitar for others. We all need serenity each and every day. Onus is on us to make sure we find some. It is worth to mention again that my therapist encouraged me to do three things each day just for me. It is hard when you never did this before but we are deserving of it that is for sure. We should not sell ourselves short anymore.

Maybe it is a special location that just brings you such support and energy. This is a place where calmness prevails and where a sense of serenity washes over you. This is a physical or spiritual location where all your thoughts and feelings flow easily without judgement. I have a couple of Zen type garden places to have a cup of tea a place to be with nature and to breathe deep and a great location to run or exercise outside.

Although I have adult children I do not wish to burden them with my problems or what I am working through. It does not seem fair that they should have to worry about solving my life or helping me get back on track. They are fantastic children and I am truly proud to be their Mom. Find someone you can relate to and feel safe to share things with or ask for guidance. My hope for you is that you find that special someone place or thing.

MANAGE

SHARE WITH CONFIDENCE AND PURPOSE

P resently I work through my distain for people who are not accountable for their own actions. And support groups for such are available along with counselling so I can be better armed with the coping skills to not allow a trigger to get me going. But to know that I can take a breath first before I react like the twenty four hour rule with elite sports is important. If parents are upset after the game there is a rule no talking to the coach until twenty four hours after the game. A lot of things do not look the same twenty four hours later. Some call this the cooling period. It is exactly that. It is an opportunity to relook at things and usually after cooling down or coming down nothing is quite as bad as it seems. Even a ten minute break changes how you look at something.

> She made broken look beautiful and strong look invincible. She walked with the Universe on her shoulders and made it look like a pair of wings.
>
> -Ariana

28

There are a lot of options to connect with people other than family, friends and work. If you are looking for more support or some support it means you are ready to go out. You are ready to meet new people or a new person. You are at the next stage of wanting to manage this new found confidence that is growing in you. Remember to congratulate yourself. Here are some places to give ideas of where you might go to find support within your neighbourhood or community.

1. Referral from your Doctor for
    a. depression
    b. abuse
    c. anxiety
    d. look at natural options
2. Local public health system
3. Local community support groups and programs
4. Sports and hobby groups
5. Government support groups

6. Organizational support groups at all levels of government
7. Centers for help in your community
8. Shelters for the abused
9. Local library for reading materials on the subject
10. A trusted family member
11. A trusted member of your community like a school teacher or boss
12. A trusted friend
13. Your community at large
14. Your place of worship
15. Universe
16. Divine

Ability to autocorrect in life will allow us to keep what is working but change what is not? Try new things. Test it out. If you need to change it up change it up. Be aware of what your voice sounds like in the mix of other voices. To be able to hear one's own voice is okay but to also hear it with others is good too. To not go overboard and command and be the only voice that is heard is not good either. There is a check and balance with voice to ensure it is speaking with love. We come from different places but we all want love and so we should be willing to give love freely in order that we get love back freely in return. In giving love freely to all we get more love back then we would ever know what to do with. It is a beautiful cycle that you do not want to break. So it is important to check your voice check your love and keep them on a healing path.

Do not speak harmful words if you do not wish to have mean or harmful words spoken to you. We are the mirror in our life. We do truly get what we give out. Do not be afraid to look in the mirror each day and love it or be honest enough to address it and fix it. Spread the sunshine and receive the sunshine but most of all be the sunshine you are. Kind be kind or kind onto kind goes a long way.

Working through the *personal progression plan* and your deepest desire story may give some ideas of where you might reach out to start sharing you. Maybe it is a sports team you always wanted to join. A new career you want to get into. The new found confidence to take a course or show your creative side or get involved with your community or church is just waiting for you. Whatever that looks like spread those wings and soar with your head held high. You are well on your way to succeeding.

BEAUTIFUL WITH YOUR FULL VOICE

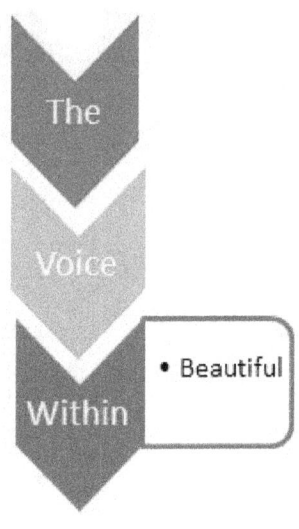

Voice with purpose is powerful[29]

ALIVE INSIDE
BEGINS WITH YOU

Once you are fully aware that you are all you need. You are enough and you love all of you in all its glory both in the past and present the possibilities for the future are endless. If you can dream it you can see it through. I have had a long time to think hard about my possibilities. I know one hundred percent my deepest desire my deepest longing my boon is centered on world peace and my vision for a foundation surrounding that. I am not sure exactly how it will play out but I do know what it looks like. I already created that vision at least one million times in my head. The journey towards that began with this book of finding, igniting and sharing hundreds of thousand lost voices never heard before like yours. You can only imagine the natural high I am on. My unique notable talent I have had all my life is that I am a cheerleader of people life brand and world. Always have been and always will be. With more clarity and way more determination, drive and resolve than ever before.

Please do keep your health, safety and wellbeing as your priority for without it we can never be as good as we were intended to be. Understanding the natural neurochemicals that are in our brain and having them produce the way they are intended manages so much of our wellbeing in the natural process. Proper sleep, diet, hydration and exercise help manage everyday aches. For those who live with chronic and severe pain everyday my heart aches for you. Sleep drives everything and is important. My hope is that you are receiving medical help and attention to mitigate the agony as best as possible in the fashion best suited for you.

We need to remain of strong body mind and soul throughout the rest of our lives. This represents the new point of ground-zero for all of us.

Alive to me means green and living. Just as we the animal creature kingdom and nature kingdom are alive, living and connected. Science says we grow new cells every single day. Our lives are in a constant metamorphic state. We are changing and evolving each hour and minute of each day and this is so exciting.

The most important thing though is to rejoice about voice where ever you are in your journey. The sound of beautiful music in full wonder and splendor is the sound of you. Celebrate every day. Remind yourself how far you have come. Never lose sight of that. Leave that old critic on the sideline for good. Wonder at the merriment and glee that is in front of you. As if you were in your car leave the rear view mirror behind you and concentrate on the big front window that is ahead of you. It is a road trip. Who cares where you have been it is all about where you are going.

Do not limit your possibilities and the ability to be alive for the first time. Everything before us is endless we are only limited by our own mind.

ANGER AT BAY

MOVING ON

Outrage will try to rear its ugly head time and time again. That rush of emotions. A quick reaction can get me in trouble all the time. Meeting rage with rage never works. Meet anger or frustration with kindness and patience is the only solution. I work hard and I am vigilant on this reactionary action.

Other people will try and drag you into their ugly because you are way too happy. Like a moth to a flame they want what you have. Try not to get sucked in it is very easy though. If you lose track and slip back into the dark revert back to light and some of the tips about loving self. Get in love with you again and again as many times as it takes. It is a repeat as required. No prescription required. Remember it is about maintaining this love for life not attaining it and moving on.

A check and balance along the way is a good thing too. Have a moment and try and listen to the sound of your voice. Is it too prominent is it over powering is it too loud is it selfish is it sharing with others is it empathetic to others or have you taken over? Remind yourself to listen. Remember all those great grandmother stories such as it is harder to listen than to speak and that is why we have two ears and only one mouth. Do not, I repeat do not beat yourself up if maybe your voice is a bit too loud. Just recognize be aware and make the adjustments that need to be made. I have had to correct my voice a couple of times throughout life. We have not had as much practice as others with our voice this is new to us. Life will be a continual try and auto correct as this is part of being alive and having a voice. Based on what we know today we try this but tomorrow we know more so we make the alterations towards more happiness and more exhilaration and off we go again.

I monitor closely what triggers my anger. Usually it is a flashback or a brief pity party. Time to take a step back and reflect on the big picture and what is important. Redirect the negative energy towards your dream. I try hard to not allow myself to get sucked in to someone else's insecurity. Again being more aware of the side effects abuse has had on our lives.

You may be at different stages and steps for a while recognize it and when you need a refresher or when you need professional help do so in order to stay on course.

GIFT OF VOICE

WITH PURPOSE

With full voice I am so excited to experience the rest of my life. I waste no time with my new conviction now for I have clearer direction. My mission my vision is created. My compass or my road map of life is created and now each idea and deepest desire I have moving forward must measure up against them. I shall not get lost anytime soon. If you have not had a chance to spend some quality time getting to know yourself better I do strongly suggest this is a great place to jump in. If the actions and interactions you do daily are not propelling you to your goal the energy you expend is for not. Yes it can still be good energy but not as purposeful as it can be and it is not helping you get nearer to your deepest desire.

Time is of the essence. The clock of life is ticking and it is running out. What will you stand for? What will your legacy in life be? Will you leave an impact on life, family and friends? It is very precious you should not waste a second more. I realize that double time now. Once it gets clearer nothing else matters but your true calling. Mine is to find and ignite voices and so I shall. They said it could not be done and I said watch me try and help make people and the world more whole and help all in it find peace.

I cannot wait to see and hear about what you are doing with your special gifts bestowed upon only you. The world needs everyone and their special gifts. The world needs you.

OPEN TO RECEIVE

LISTEN HEAR TOUCH FEEL TASTE SMELL AND SEE

Reignite with self and Universe or find the connection for the first time. Forewarned is forearmed and now once you have come to the light side you cannot subject yourself to the dark side again. Certainly we are aware of the terrible detriment the dark side has on our well-being and our existence. There is no going back to the dark side only forward towards the bright shining light of you.

With our new ability to listen hear touch feel taste smell and see we are awakened to what the world truly has to offer and give. Our senses are heightened and honed to the deepest degree of awareness and it is so enlightening and stunningly beautiful. I am seeing for the first time in my life.

Previously I did not understand what the goose bumps and shivers meant in my life. Being spiritually connect I do now. I have great feeling and I know that for me this is affirmation and guidance or the hand of the Universe wishing to show me that I am on the right path. The

Universe does not wish for us to fail it wishes that we succeed. Please remember that it presents to us just who and what we need when we need it. If we are open to receive the message. The old me had doubt and would not follow. The new me is confident in the beautiful path in front of me and there is no bumping me off this road no matter how bumpy or windy it gets.

Glorious reader it is time to rejoice and to really understand the feeling you are having of euphoria and over the moon with glee is now the new normal. The Universe really wants you to feel this good so you can fulfil your first deepest desire your dream and calling.

For me who has always been so connected to Universe even from a small child it is important I understand now this is affirmation from the Universe. It is such an amazing feeling to know you are on the right path. It is the release of natural chemicals in our brain that put me on a permanent high for life. For everyone connection with life force is different and that is the true miracle. It is to be truly alive with motive with full voice with no fear. To be open to receive what the Universe has to offer and has always had. This is simply amazing.

The world needs your voice to be heard. It is part of the balance and equation. Without it we are not as whole as we are supposed to be. You are the missing link the world needs. There is great solace in understanding that we do stand in unity with the world in that we are all seeking joy and happiness. The world needs everyone.

FIND IGNITE SHARE
OTHER MISSING VOICES

I have seen a lot in this Universe, World, Country, Province, City, Town, Community, work and family. But I have also missed a lot that was there all the time. I see all the colours of the world the people and places but now I just see them better. I am more equipped to manage my life. I am thankful for the guidance of above and friends who helped me arrive here.

I am so excited to create the new me and to watch me grow and learn and to see how far and exactly where I will go in my life. What type of impact I may create on life and for the world and what will be my legacy to leave my family and the Universe. Ultimately what will they say about me at my funeral. What did I stand for and how will I be eulogized? That speech has yet to be fully written. I want it to say she found lots of voices along the way some lost some already found each beautiful and she honoured each and every one of them for their individuality. I wish this for you too.

Everything changes and does not stay the same nor should we. Our lives are in a constant state of metamorphosis. Trust you are where you are supposed to be and be who you were intended to be with a full voice. Oh more shivers what a way to end with affirmation from above it does not get any better than that.

Find your voice, ignite your voice and share your voice.

Standing Tall One Voice at a Time

APPENDIX A
REFLECTIVE QUOTES

30

31

APPENDIX A: REFLECTIVE QUOTES

32

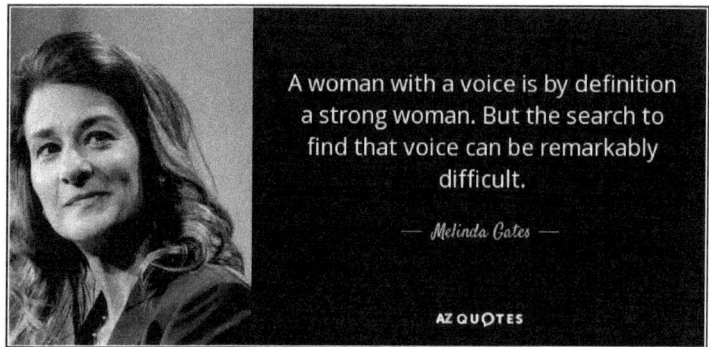

APPENDIX B

CHARTS AND RESOURCES

33

THE HIGH COST OF SEXUAL VIOLENCE

When a woman is sexually assaulted, the impact on her life can last for months—even years—and it can affect her education, employment, and long-term well-being. Society pays, too. In Canada, the annual costs of sexual assault and related offences for the criminal justice system, social services, and employers add up to an estimated $200 million. When you include the medical costs, lost productivity, and pain and suffering of victims, the cost skyrockets to $4.8 billion. The problem is huge. In a 2009 Statistics Canada survey, 472,000 people in Canada reported they had been sexually assaulted. Supports such as counselling and legal advice help victims re-establish a sense of safety and control over their lives, and reduce the long-term collective costs. But to stop the violence—for good—we also need to invest in violence prevention programs that teach young people to understand how to give and receive consent, and how to create healthier relationships. LEARN MORE
CANADIANWOMEN.ORG/STOP-THE-VIOLENCE

THE FIGURES IN FOCUS
The aftermath of sexual assault amounts to an estimated $4.8 billion per year. Here are some of the costs incurred:

COSTS TO VICTIMS
Medical — $113 Million
Lost Productivity — $211 Million
Pain and Suffering — $4.3 Billion

COSTS TO SOCIETY
Criminal Justice System — $150 Million
Social Services — $32 Million
Employer Losses — $18 Million

SOURCE: DEPARTMENT OF JUSTICE CANADA, 2009

CANADIAN WOMEN'S FOUNDATION
canadianwomen.org

APPENDIX B: CHARTS AND RESOURCES

34

LESS THAN 10% of sexual assaults are reported to the police

460,000 ANNUAL NUMBER OF SEXUAL ASSAULTS REPORTED IN NATIONAL SURVEY

15,200 REPORTED TO THE POLICE

13,200 RECORDED AS A CRIME

5,544 CHARGES LAID

2,824 PROSECUTED

1,519 CONVICTED

LOST VOICE

LOST VOICE GROUP DISCUSSION QUESTIONS [36]

	YES	NO
Do you live with a controlling figure in your life and is isolation a factor? If so are you able to explain in what way?	( )	( )
Are you the target of constant put downs, yelling, name calling or swearing? How does that make you feel inside and how are you managing?	( )	( )
Are you made to feel small in public and insignificant? If so how?	( )	( )

Sometimes it is like walking on eggshells. What are the things that can turn your day into a walking time bomb?

Have you ever feared for your life, please explain:

Where does your pain and hurt stem from?

What is stopping you from loving all of you?

Finish the sentence: If I could do anything in the world I would

Answering yes to any question would mean you should talk with a professional about how you are feeling and being treated in this relationship or others in your life. Also work on getting to a safe place and learning to love all of you more.

Visit **DebbieMajor.ca** for free training to benefit you in your journey of love of self and finding your full voice.
More information can be found on the back cover.

ACKNOWLEDGEMENTS

To my husband a unique bond and love hold us together. Our journey of exploring more who we are together brings tremendous joy excitement and wonder to my heart for all things to revel in and explore moving forward. In solo we are polar opposites in togetherness we are the recipe for a perfect ying yang. Continued willingness on both of our parts to be open and grow with each new learn trial or experience in life and to taking our love and respect of each other to new places and heights.

To my Mother without her steadfast love and ability to show firsthand what it is to compromise self for sake of others and to help thy neighbour with want for nothing in return. She taught that love is in us to give freely and that each day is a present. She is eighty eight years young this year.

To my Father who is watching from heaven and I say I got this Dad and he would answer back giver heck boy giver heck! So to my Dad I say what I said in 1999.

Ode to Dad
I'll love you now
I'll love you always
I'll love you when
you're here and then

You make me proud
to be your daughter
you make me proud
to be your friend

You are my Dad
today and then

To my brothers and sisters, their families, a cousin, my husband's family and my inner circle of friends my love for them is unconditional. I am honoured by your encouragement, support and your presence in my life.

To Kary Oberbrunner who was the pivotal turning point in my life. His ability and desire to move people to action with purpose and towards their desire is his gift within. I do not think he realizes the full extent of how many lives he has changed, saved and enriched just by being who he was intended to be.

To a very unique group of girlfriends who have a large placeholder in my heart, forever Six Ten! Many of the decisions to arrive at this place in my life stem from the sharing of experiences and the ability to talk freely with no judgement. Six Ten is both a physical and mental place of being. Yielding and encouraging pure acceptance of where one is at in life with no preconceptions. A place where true love and kindness will always be at the door to greet you and welcome you!

ACKNOWLEDGEMENTS

For my editors Heather Parker-Nance and Kathy Smith without their support my true purpose in life would not have been realized so eloquently. I will forever be indebted to their generous love and support.

To my health partner in crime the scenery and the rugged terrain and hills we traversed on our miles and miles of walks and dragging our butts to the gym four times a week for over four years could not hold a candle to the journey our hearts took beside each other. To all the cares and worries of the world we solved and shared and too many more. I cannot wait to see you in the red dress.

To Donna Staub whom the Universe so kindly bestowed a reconnection of two kindred hearts recently after being apart for too long. I rejoice in pure wonder of this and am thankful. Her guidance and uncanny timing of events is not by happen stance but exactly where the Divine has put our two hearts for ever intertwined. I am honoured for her guidance in my life.

To myself I am proud of my courage and strength to arrive at this place in my life. To my new found liberation and freedom and where it will take me on the rest of my journey. Here is to being alive and aware of the Universe its beauty and all its offerings in whole for the first time. I am a miracle as we all are and I rejoice bask and bath in this every day. To myself I promise to endeavour to spread love and kindness for as long as I live. To remember that we all have benefit to give and that we are all created equal. There is no one story or journey more important than another. That there is enough for everyone, we should not exclude anyone and we can all get along and share.

To our Universe we acknowledge all of its beauty and we respect that it is in our care.

DOCUMENTATION AND RESEARCH

1. Major, Debbie. 2017 Introduction Poem "Bruised and Broken"
2. Major, Debbie. 2017 Part I Poem "A Home is Where the Heart Is"
3. Picture Quotes *Inspirational Quotes.* "Feeling Invisible"
4. Romeo, Tony. 1970. *The Partridge Family Album.* "I Think I Love You". # 1 Billboard Hot 100 1970, https://en.wikipedia.org/wiki/I_Think_I_Love_You May 21 2017
5. Anglin, Perry 1984 Referral Letter Revenue Canada Taxation
6. Canadian Women's Foundation, *Infographic-Violence.* "Should I Stay or Should I Go" http://www.canadianwomen.org may 21, 2017
7. Major, Debbie. 1977 Grade Nine High School
8. Major, Debbie. 1979 Graduation Picture Grade Eleven High School
9. Centre for Therapy Kingston ON. info@centrefortherapy.ca http://centrefortherapy.ca
10. Rich, Charlie - Singer. 1973 *Behind Closed Doors* Kenny O'Dell writer https://en.wikipedia.org/wiki/Behind_Closed_Doors
11. Major, Debbie. 2000. Songwriter Composer. "*Baby You Can't Have My Thoughts*"

12. Groom, Winston. 1986. *Forrest Gump:* The Novel that inspired the Academy Award-Winning Film. New York, USA: Random House. Roth, Eric 1994. *Tom Hanks is Forrest Gump:* The world will never be the same once you've seen it through the eyes of Forrest Gump
13. Obrebrunner, Kary 2016. *Elixir Project Elixir Project Experience.* Ohio: AAE http://elixirprojectexperience.com 2016. "RAS Filter"
14. Obrebrunner, Kary. 2016. *Elixir Project – Elixir Project Experience* Ohio: AAE http://elixirprojectexperience.com 2016. "BED Model"
15. Major, Debbie 2017 *KindbKind*
16. Unknown. 2017. Inspirational Quote: "*Strong is the Only Choice*"
17. Major, Debbie Part II *Poem* "Spreading Love"
18. Canadian Women's Foundation. *Infographic.* "What is Happening to Our Girls" http://www.canadianwomen.org
19. Anger Management Resources. Dr. William DeFoore, PH D. http://angermanagementresources.com
20. Major, Debbie. 1998 *Play Fair, Share, Be Nice*
21. Obrebrunner, Kary. 2016. *Elixir Project* Elixir Project Experience Ohio: AAE http://www.elixirprojectexperience.com 2016
22. Jobs, Steve. 2005. *Commencement Address (2005) – Stanford News.* "Connect The Dots Speech"
23. Young, Neil. 1977. *Find The Cost of Freedom*
24. Canadian Women's Foundation. *Infographic* "The Need" http://www.canadianwomen.org
25. Canadian Association for Equality http://www.EqualityCanada.ca
26. Corporate World – "*SWOT*" Strengths, Weaknesses, Opportunities Threat Analysis

DOCUMENTATION AND RESEARCH

27. Obrebrunner, Kary. 2013 *The Deeper Path:* Five Steps That Let Your Hurts Lead to Healing Grand Rapids, MI: Baker Books. http://www.deeperpathbook.com
28. Unknown. Ariana. *Inspirational quote:* Broken look Beautiful
29. Major, Debbie. Part III *Poem* "Voice is Powerful"
30. Languag, C. *Mind over Matter. Inspirational Quote:* "Be who you were created to be" 2017
31. Hemingway, Ernest. *Inspirational Quote* Princess in the Tower. "The World Breaks Everyone" http://princessinthetower.org/contact/
32. Gates, Melinda. *Quote:* A Woman with a Voice is by Definition a Strong Woman. http://www.gatesfoundation.org/
33. Canadian Women's Foundation *Infographic* "The High Cost of Sexual Violence" http://www.canadianwomen.org
34. Canadian Women's Foundation *Infographic* "Less than 10% of sexual assaults are reported to the police." http://www.canadianwomen.org
35. Canadian Women's Foundation. *Infographic* "What is Happening to our Girls" http://www.canadianwomen.org
36. Major, Debbie. July 2017. *Lost Voice* "Group Discussion Questions"
37. Scott Grant Photography. 2016 *Picture* Ottawa Redblacks Alumni Cheer Game, Aug 2016. TD Place Ottawa, ON http://www.imagecommunications.ca/about/
38. Panchal, Paresh SK photography *Picture* "Head Shot Back Cover" http://www.facebook.com/skgraphix.org/
39. Vukovic, Estella 99Designs *Book Cover* stella_e https://99designs.ca/users/1386441/contact

Cheerleader people brand world
37 38 39

ABOUT DEBBIE

Debbie Major's purpose and deepest desire in life is to ensure those without confidence especially the young and vulnerable find love and respect of self, realize their worth, and ultimately discover the voice within their lost voice. In hopes they may share their message with the world. An Author, Coach, and Keynote Speaker she earned a Bachelor of Commerce Honours from the University of Ottawa and graduated Cum Laude with a Marketing and Finance degree in 1986. She had her own dance studio and taught classical ballet and modern jazz at the age of twenty one. She was a Rhythm Rider a Professional Cheerleader with the Ottawa Rough Riders of the Canadian Football League also called The CFL for five years and enjoyed her role as Captain culminating in attending a Grey Cup in 1981. She is a Cheerleader of life people brand and world. Pursuing her marketing career for over twenty five years she is successful in her role as President of a multi-million dollar direct marketing company. Serving three not for profit boards close to her heart collectively for more than thirty years including receiving a Life Time Honorary Membership with one of the not for profit organizations. She enjoys the Universe and all its wonder and magic it has to offer. Debbie and her husband live near Toronto Ontario and are blessed with an amazing daughter and son.

YOU HAVE READ MY STORY FROM HURT TO ALIVE.

ARE YOU READY TO CREATE YOUR STORY AND END YOUR SUFFERING?

ARE YOU READY TO BELIEVE IN YOURSELF?

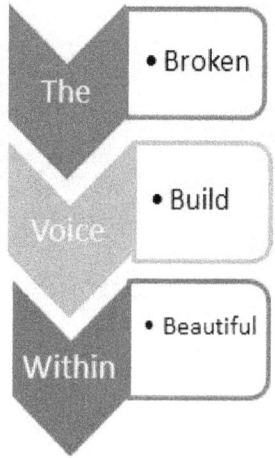

Define

Describe

Differentiate

COURAGE|CONCEIVE|COMPOSE|CREATE|CLARIFY|CORRECT|COMMUNICATE|CELEBRATE

**IT IS TIME FOR YOU TO FIND YOUR VOICE AND HAVE A SAY.
ACCESS YOUR FREE TRAINING TODAY SO THAT YOU CAN:**

Stop the pain.
Get to a safe place.
Live a positive self-image.
Deliver a clear message in life and at work.
Connect with Debbie at **DebbieMajor.ca**

www.ingramcontent.com/pod-product-compliance
Lightning Source LLC
LaVergne TN
LVHW011825060526
838200LV00053B/3904